FIFTY YEARS IN MY BOOKSTORE

OR A LIFE WITH BOOKS

by Harry W. Schwartz

With a Foreword by A. David Schwartz

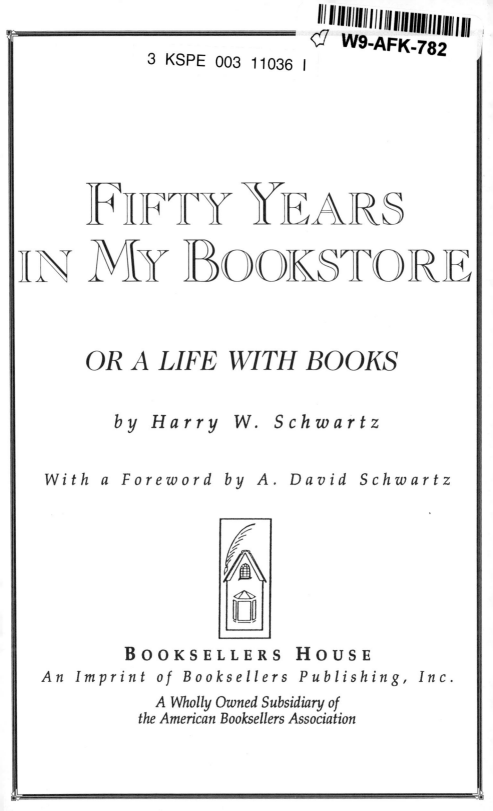

BOOKSELLERS HOUSE
An Imprint of Booksellers Publishing, Inc.
A Wholly Owned Subsidiary of
the American Booksellers Association

BOOKSELLERS HOUSE

An imprint of Booksellers Publishing, Inc.

A wholly owned subsidiary of the
American Booksellers Association
560 White Plains Road
Tarrytown, NY 10591
(914) 631-7800, (800) 637-0037

Cover Design: Ira Cook
Book Design: Linda Miller

ISBN: 1-879923-03-3

First Booksellers House Printing, April 1992

Printed in the United States of America

To my wife Reva
and son David

WITHOUT WHOSE ENCOURAGEMENT
THESE REMINISCENCES
WOULD NOT HAVE BEEN POSSIBLE
AND
TO ALL THE GREAT BOOKLOVERS
FRIENDS AND CUSTOMERS
I HAVE ENJOYED
THROUGH THE YEARS

CONTENTS

FOREWORD

As the reader will learn, Harry Schwartz came to book-selling at a relatively early age, after a youth filled with adventure and wandering. When he found bookselling, it became a passion beyond all else except possibly for his bookselling companion, his wife.

Bookselling was the ultimate occupation, before which other callings were, if not drudgery, at least dull. Bookselling, to Harry Schwartz, was noble and faultless, moral and lifegiving, challenging and exciting, "an occupation for gentlemen," but one that held no barriers to those of any class. In short, as I, his only child, was often told, bookselling was the only conceivable livelihood to adopt.

What will also become apparent to the reader is that Harry Schwartz was a curious mixture of rebellion and conservativism. He rejected organized religion, yet maintained his cultural definitions; rejected capitalism, yet was a shrewd and aggressive businessman. He had very high standards for what he read, yet he would sell almost any book to any person who showed the slightest interest. For a man so proud of his chosen universe, it constantly shocked me to hear him telling his customers boldfaced lies while making his recommendations.

A child growing up in this milieu would find it easy to identify the totems to rebel against, particularly when those totems were not only constantly prayed to, but exalted above all else.

As befit a son of a shopkeeper's son, I began work in the basement of the bookstore untwisting rope and salvaging cardboard, which I reused when packaging customers' books for the parcel post. By the age of eighteen I had seen enough and heard more than enough of the glories of the book business to be in almost constant rebellion against the world's most glorious profession.

I watched Harry Schwartz, now approaching his thirtieth year in the shop, becoming increasingly crusty with his old customers and downright rude to his new ones. Six- and seven-day work weeks with only one-week vacation a year didn't add to the job's attraction, yet my father never wavered from either his own enthusiasm or his insistence that I become a bookseller. This contest continued for years. Years of quiet terror during the McCarthy fifties when I wondered if the shop would be picketed and my father called before the House's Unamerican Activities Committee. Years of resisting censorship while carefully keeping the balance between a "serious" shop and one that gleefully sold hundreds of copies of *Tropic of Cancer*, not for its literary merit, but because the good burghers of Milwaukee wanted to read a "dirty book."

And if the truth be known, the son was losing the struggle to the father. After graduating from the university and working in New York City bookshops, I joined him, becoming his reluctant assistant and ever-willing critic. I pushed him into doing what I had always heard from him was possible—using books as a social tool to change the world.

Under his watchful and somewhat fearful eye the bookshop engaged itself in the civil rights and anti-Vietnam war movements. I learned that these were not new departures for Harry Schwartz, as he had used the bookshop to raise money to aid the republican side in the Spanish Civil War. So it was by gradual and constant struggle that the father's ideas and opinions were passed on to the son.

One final conflict remained. Because I was raised to regard socialism as the solution for mankind I questioned what my father and I were doing in this most capitalistic of enterprises. By the end of the sixties, with Richard Nixon running America, and after reading Sinclair Lewis' *Babbit,* I fled the shop for a commune in Maine from whence I could really remake the world. My father, nearly broken-hearted, couldn't believe the folly of leaving a prospering bookshop to cut pulpwood in down east Maine. However, such a job had he performed on me that I was back in Milwaukee a year to the day of leaving.

Now Harry Schwartz played his final ace. He told his son, "...the next time you leave this shop to search or to play, you leave your own shop." That was 1972, and Harry Schwartz was true to his word. Quietly assisting and giving advice only when called upon, Harry Schwartz secretly glowed that his son had finally understood that bookselling was an occupation to glory in, be proud of, and a way to remake the world in one's own image. And the son loved his father for it.

A. David Schwartz

A. David Schwartz in a modern-day Harry W. Schwartz Bookshop, a business founded by his father.

PREFACE

W hen Don Olesen of the Milwaukee Journal *asked to write an article on me for* Insight Magazine, *I did not realize, at the time, that this would result in a splendid introduction to the book I was writing on my bookselling experiences.*

Some of these experiences have not been pleasant, as the reader of this book will discover, and one will inevitably conclude that bookselling is not the easiest method of earning a livelihood. In fact, of all the professions, and bookselling surely is a profession, it is probably the most difficult.

But there were other compensations besides bread and butter that have made this fifty-year journey worthwhile, and which I hope I have described adequately. There never was the slightest deviation from my choice of bookselling. Not even during the worst of the depression years was there any question whether I would remain a bookseller. Thus, despite my frequently severe indictment of many of the shapes and forms of bookselling, I can sincerely state that if I had to live it all over again, I would perform it largely as I have described it in the book you are about to read.

H. W. S.

Milwaukee 1977

Reva and I at our home in Fox Point.

INTRODUCTION

*Retired but Not on the Shelf**

By Don Olesen

H arry W. Schwartz does not like best seller lists. He also has an aversion to speed reading, censors, chain bookstores and the ungentle, unintellectual world of book publishing today. At root, Schwartz is a warm, positive sort of man. But after 47 years in the bookselling business, he does have a few peeves.

Schwartz's love affair with books is a lifetime thing. He is an intellectual whose formal schooling ended with high school. He writes articles. He collects rare books. Like the literary gentlemen of gentler times, he has corresponded with fine writers down the years; people like William Faulkner, the reclusive B. Traven (most widely known for *The Treasure of Sierra Madre*), Vardis Fisher (*Children of God*), Aleister Crowley (author, poet, magician, mountain climber, mystic, Satanist).

The bookseller is lean, fit, feisty and 71. He uses the Queen's English with elegance. He is that vanishing figure in a mob of Philistine hustlers, a genuine man of letters.

Schwartz also is a canny businessman for whom the career of selling books has been quite decently rewarding; witness

---

* Reprinted by permission from the Milwaukee *Journal,* November 24, 1974.

the pretty stone and shingle Schwartz home on a winding drive in Fox Point.

When I called there not long ago, the bookseller was firmly planted on the screened porch hammering out his autobiography on a venerable typewriter (nonelectric). "It's one of those endless things," he explained. "I've written 60,000 words so far." Said he felt a little like Penelope in Homer's Ulysses. (Penelope, you'll recall, promised to choose among her impatient suitors once she finished weaving a shroud for Laertes; for three years she wove by day and unraveled what she wove by night.) "Each day I throw away the old stuff and insert the new."

Capsule biography (in considerably fewer than 60,000 words): Harry W. Schwartz graduated from Milwaukee's Washington High in 1921 and promptly hit the road, "bumming" (his word) around the country. In Los Angeles he met his future at the Holmes Book Store. Here he followed intellectual pursuits, such as sweeping floors and filling up the nickel book bins on the sidewalk outside the store (no book costing more than 5 cents). "The job was menial but I loved it; I found I had an affinity for books."

He eventually followed his affinity back to Milwaukee and opened his first bookstore in 1927, in partnership with one Paul Romaine, who later sold out his share. "It was on a shoestring," Schwartz recalled. "All we had between us was our personal libraries; we borrowed money from my mother to pay the express charges for our first shipment of books."

That first store, Casanova Book Sellers, was at 2611 N. Downer Ave., a site now occupied by a Sentry Food Store. Schwartz moved his business downtown in 1937, eventually landing on his present site in 1950 and expanding there 10 years later. He formally "retired" in 1972, selling the business to his son David. Harry Schwartz still works part time. He is "sort of helping out."

End of capsule biography. On to the opinions, prejudices and deeds of a man of letters in the book jungle.

There are cycles in reader tastes just as marked as cycles in fashion, Schwartz says. "There are periods when you have men's shirts with high collars and periods with low collars. There are narrow ties and now big ties, and the same thing is true with books." (His voice is husky, almost gravelly.)

Sometimes the historical novel rides high, and sometimes "you couldn't get rid of an historical novel, nobody would touch it." Or poetry. "For a long time you couldn't sell a line of poetry in this country, and then it came into a big, strong vogue; and then you had another period of completely ignoring poetry."

The same with fiction, a sort of tidal ebb and flow. "The only thing that has maintained itself, kept a uniform demand, has been the mystery story. The good writers have become household words. S. S. Van Dine, Rex Stout, Agatha Christie, Dorothy Sayers. And the demand for Western stories is pretty constant, too."

Since World War II, there has been a sparkling boom in technical and 'how to' books. Years ago, only libraries and big institutions bought them; the average bookstore didn't have a technical department. "But now, with the era of electronics and all the gadgets that we have, the number of technical and 'how to' books is legion. There used to be a little magazine that dealt with new books coming out on technical subjects. This magazine was about 150 pages in size. Now this thing has grown into a volume this thick (he illustrates with his fingers)—about 4,000 pages.

"We first went into technical books in 1940. Before that we didn't carry a one, but I could see the war coming along and I knew there would be a demand for these books. I put in a small selection. And we built up a business which is now one of the big areas of our whole store."

Science fiction books are selling merrily today; "it is just incredible, especially for the young." And current events. "Years ago, dead. Today it's off the press almost before it happens. Woodward and Bernstein. There also has been an upsurge in sports books in the past 20 years or so. Pro football, for instance. I think now that we've got too many on that subject; we're overdoing it."

Which leads Schwartz to discuss the overkill in publishing. "This is one of the things in the book business (his two hands chop the air). You jump on the bandwagon, everybody gets on. And pretty soon, if somebody sells one book there are 10 books on the subject. I've advocated a clearinghouse so that if Publisher A knows Publisher B is doing a book on Frank Sinatra, A won't do one or will hold back. But they say, 'Schwartz, you're crazy, we can't wait for anybody. Besides, tell him to hold his book back, not mine.'" He cackles his high-pitched he-he-he-he.

And Book Publishing?

"From being a nice literary, quiet, gentle business, publishing has changed into a rough, competitive, amazingly fecund operation. It ceased to be a gentle humanitarian, intellectual business about 15 or 20 years ago...."

Paperback books are a profitable part of this rough, competitive, fecund business, but it wasn't always so. Schwartz remembers when he couldn't give away a paperback, and he was in on the very beginnings. It was 1939. Paperbacks were quite new in England and an untested novelty in this country. A Milwaukee man with a printing plant and "quite a bit of money—I don't want to mention his name—" returned from a European trip and marched into Schwartz's store, full of steam.

"He said, Mr. Schwartz, I just came back from Europe where I saw these tremendous paperbacks called Penguin Books. Why can't they publish something like this in America? What do I do? I said, well, you do two things. First of all get hold of a bundle of money and second get hold of some books. He says, I've got the money; how do I get the books? I suggested 25 big selling books, of which he picked 12. They were all tremendous titles. And he got the rights and published them for 25 cents each. He printed 10,000 copies of each title. They were called Red Arrow Books. I was the man in the background."

Mr. X had display racks made. He got national distribution of his paperbacks. "It was the biggest fiasco you ever heard of in your life. It was a dreadful thing. He hardly sold a book. He was ahead of his time. Luckily he was a very wealthy man because he dropped $100,000, and in those days it would be like dropping a million today."

Pocket Books, another new United States publisher of paperbacks, fared better than Red Arrow; eventually it prospered. But not in 1939 at the Schwartz Bookshop. Pocket Books sent a salesman around to see the bookseller. "He said, we're publishing paperbacks, 25 cents each. They were all tremendous titles like 'How to Win Friends and Influence People.' There were mysteries, everything. He said, we'll furnish you with a big gondola—a rack—that will hold 1,000 books. I said forget it, save your breath, I don't want anything to do with it. So he said, look, you are the only likely person in Milwaukee to buy these books. I've got to sell them somewhere, so I'll make a deal with you. You buy the books and don't pay for them for six months. We'll give you the gondola and 1,000 books. Try them.

"So I said, okay. And, as I surmised, no sales. People would come in, look at this thing, walk around it and walk away." (Schwartz acted out this little drama for me, stalking around an imaginary display rack and frowning mightily.) "People just simply wouldn't touch them."

Why was the public reluctant to buy good books at bargain prices? "It was something so new, so startling, so completely unlike anything they'd experienced in books. The novelty was way out of their experience."

Paperbacks eventually did catch on, of course. By the 1950s they were selling nicely. In the early days they were perhaps 1 percent to 2 percent of Schwartz's volume; today, almost a third.

If the bookseller's business is books, his pleasure is reading. When he and Reva moved to their Fox Point home in 1968, 86 *cases* of books moved in with them. Walls of rooms both upstairs and down are walled with books. The house wears the rich aroma of books.

When Schwartz comes upon fine writing in his reading he pauses to savor words and phrases and paragraphs; to read and reread them. Thus he detests the modern cult of speed reading. "It misses the whole quality, the flavor of the writing."

He also dislikes best seller book lists, which may ring oddly when coming from a bookseller. "Actually I hate the best seller lists because they limit the peoples' ability to make a selection for themselves," he says. (Both hands make little chopping motions again.) "What's everybody else reading? Get on the bandwagon! You don't have any fun picking your own books. You don't even allow bookstores to make a suggestion. I think they're horrible."

Schwartz also views censorship with caustic distaste. "First of all I might give you what is my credo (right hand sweeping, palm up). I don't believe in censorship, No. 1, I think it is almost impossible to censor ideas. You'll be in a tangle from which you can't extricate yourself; just a complete semantic brawl with no conclusion.

"Then also I feel morally that a person should be allowed to read whatever he wants to read. Ethically, intellectually, there should be no attempt to tell him, or to force him, or to suggest that he cannot read something.

"Sometimes it becomes such a farcical thing that it's very hard to understand how people of normal intelligence can get mixed up in it. Let me give you an example. In 1949 came a book called 'Mr. Roberts' (by Thomas Heggen). It is a very clean book." It was withdrawn from sale in Milwaukee at the request of the district attorney's office, which called the book "obscene and filthy." Why? "Profanity," Schwartz said. "Damns, hells, sonovabitches. In the context of today, this would be Sunday school reading."

Anyway, Schwartz was asked by the book's publisher to be a guinea pig in a court test case to fight the ban. He would sell the book and get arrested. The publisher's lawyers would defend him. If the book were judged obscene he'd go to jail. Schwartz agreed. "I'd been shooting off my mouth all these years and now I certainly would be a fool to miss an opportunity to do something for the ideas I'd been espousing." But the test never occurred. The DA's office had second thoughts and lifted the ban before Schwartz could get himself arrested.

Censorship, Schwartz feels, reached a pinnacle of absurdity in Chicago where his former partner, Paul Romaine, was arrested for selling *Memoirs of a Woman of Pleasure* (better known as *Fanny Hill* by John Cleland) to a police undercover agent. Romaine was tried by jury in 1965, and Schwartz was a defense witness. Jurors were asked about their reading habits. "One person said that she had read a copy of Huxley's *Brave New World* way back in 1939 and that was the last book she had read. One person on the jury had read a book! I thought, my God, imagine a bookseller being sent to prison by such a jury!"

"Romaine was convicted. He appealed, but the case against him was dropped when the United States Supreme Court reversed a Massachusetts ban on *Fanny Hill*. And today the book is selling in paperback in every drugstore in the country. There are books published today that you wouldn't believe possible. We would have been sent to jail if we'd sold these books a couple of years ago."

As a bookseller, Schwartz views some of his "adult" bookstore neighbors with extreme distaste, but he rejects censorship here, too. "I feel very bad about some of these adult bookstores. I feel they are in very bad taste. I abhor them. But I feel that we simply have to tolerate them, otherwise we get into this field of suppression. And then there's no hope."

Schwartz sees another threat to literature, one even more subtle and potentially injurious than censorship—the chain bookstore, a creature of the postwar shopping center and the more recent shopping mall. He refers particularly to B. Dalton Bookseller (at Mayfair, Southridge, Northridge) and Walden Book Stores (Brookfield Square, Capitol Court, Northridge, Southridge). "It doesn't hurt us directly. Most of our sales are books you can't get any other place." But:

"The people at Dalton now have about 140 stores. There are plans on the drawing board for about 4,000 stores. Walden has about 500. Their projection is to have about 12,000 stores.*

---

* *Editor's Note*: At press time (April 1992), B. Dalton had approximately 750 stores, and Walden had more than 1,200.

These two are going to make it possible to have a bookstore in every community in the country. Stores already in existence there will have to either go out of business or sell out to them.

"In that sense I feel that the chain is a vicious thing because it is driving the independent bookstore out of business. My God, what's going to happen to the little bookstore? I think they're doomed (both hands raised, helplessly).

"What do we lose? I think that the chain bookstores eventually will reach a point where they can control what is being published. They'll have the ability to tell the publisher what they want, and the publisher will have to kowtow to them. They may become so big that they can determine *what* we read. I think it's going to be such a blow to the culture of this country that it will be hard to measure. The ability to select and buy books is a measure of the culture of the people."

Does this boom in books and bookstores make us a highly literate nation? The bookseller thinks not. "We publish in this country roughly about 10,000 new titles a year. But England, a country which is much smaller, publishes 30,000. Germany, West Germany alone, publishes 50,000 new books. So we are really down on the bottom of the literate list.

"We are a big nation of magazine readers and television viewers. I sometimes ask people who come into the store, what are you reading? I haven't read a book in years, they say. What do you do at night? Watch television.

"The percentage that buys books is minuscule. In a country with our wealth and our distribution facilities, it is sad...."

Postscript: After our visit, Harry and Reva Schwartz see me to the door. Just outside, among the pachysandra plants, is one of those humane traps for small animals. Chipmunks eat the pachysandra roots. Harry and Reva have nothing against chipmunks, but . . . hence the trap. When he traps a chipmunk, the sometimes caustic bookseller transports the critter five miles into the country-side and releases it.

Just a softy at heart.

November 24, 1974.

PART ONE

Beginning,
1903–1926

THE WORLD OF BOOKS

Is the most remarkable creation
of Man
Nothing else that he builds
ever lasts
Monuments fall
Nations perish
Civilizations grow old and die
And after an era of Darkness
New races build others
But in the World of Books
are volumes
That have seen this happen
again and again
And yet live on
Still young
Still as fresh
As the day they were written
Still telling men's hearts
Of the hearts of men centuries dead

CLARENCE DAY

CHAPTER I

O nce upon a time there was a little boy who read too many books. He read all the books by Jack London, Joseph Altsheler, Horatio Alger, Jr., Oliver Optick, Edward S. Ellis, Harry Castlemon, and hundreds of other writers. Once he had stumbled upon an author he did not leave him alone until he had exhausted him, or at least read every book by him in the Public Library. He identified with all the heroes in the stories. There were times when he yearned to be a sailor, a trapper, a woodsman, a hunter, and of course a writer. As a boy of twelve he wrote stories in his bedroom. Later he would read these stories to his sister and upon her advice he would tear them up. This youth did not become a writer but perhaps the next closest thing to a writer. He became a bookseller.

I was born January 27, 1903, in the small town of Berlin, Wisconsin. I remember nothing about Berlin, having lived there barely three years when my family moved to Iron Ridge, Wisconsin. Immigrating to America from Russia in about 1890, my family came directly to Berlin, where we had an uncle who had arrived some years earlier and who owned a general store there. Uncle needed young, healthy and honest people to operate the store, and how could he do better than by importing help from the same "shtetl" in which he had lived in Russia? He merely was obligated to send the passage money (steerage) and he could get all the help he would need for years to come. The family worked until the passage money had been repaid, then received a pittance in wages. In this way Uncle financed bringing our entire family from Russia to the

Promised Land. If at times they felt bitter about being exploited, or so it seemed to them, they were also grateful to Uncle for bringing them to America. And if the older children of the family (10 children) found that America was not really the land of Milk and Honey, at least they had escaped the Russian Army and the pogroms.

The general store at this time was the principal shopping facility in the small towns of America, before the automobile and the chain stores (Sears Roebuck, Montgomery Ward, etc.) drove them out of business. In the early days the general store grew from a tiny business into a sizable enterprise. In the first place there was no competition, and even if there was another store in the town, there was generally enough business for both stores to make a good livelihood. Of course it was desirable to find a town without a general store, but this could not always be discovered. My oldest brother, Louis, made his home in Hartland, Wisconsin, where he built a business from scratch into a volume of a million dollars a year. But he never lost the ways of a small merchant, and could sometimes be found in the store basement picking out the wilted leaves from the lettuce when the store was jammed with customers and he should have been attending them.

Many of these budding merchants had their origins as peddlers. A horse and wagon was their store and they went directly to their customer's home. At this time almost 90 percent of America was rural and the small farmer was the backbone of the country. It was from these small beginnings of a horse and wagon peddler that many fortunes were made. Many of these peddlers in the mid-west were of Jewish descent. They quickly adapted themselves to the life of peddling, but the most important reason why many of the immigrants became peddlers was because it required very little capital. The merchandise was generally obtained on consignment from a friendly merchant, and the only cash investment was a horse and wagon. My father began his peddling with kerosene, a commodity that every farmer needed at this time, before the widespread use of electricity. From kerosene as a beginning, he added other items and soon was able to open a small general store in Iron Ridge.

Father learned English and became acquainted with German by reading the discarded newspapers that the farmers wrapped their produce in. He was entirely self-taught and aside from a few years as a "yeshiva-bocher" had never entered a school. Father was also our delivery boy for our store, and the sight of this small, bearded man perched on the high seat of the delivery wagon seemed rather incongruous. Yet year after year he uncomplainingly performed this menial task.

Iron Ridge is a blank in my memory too, but I do recall two episodes, one of which could have had a tragic aftermath. I remember a closet in which I would be locked when I was naughty or did not obey my sisters. The closet contained a rosary which held all the terrors of hell for me. How this rosary got into the closet and why it remained there I do not know. Nor do I know why a string of beads should hold such terrors for me. The second incident that I remember occurred when I was seven or eight years old. At that time farmers carried heavy loads in what was called lumber wagons with thick plank flooring. One day, I and two friends (the three of us had played hookey from school) tried to hitch a ride on one of these wagons. I helped both of my companions onto the wagon and in attempting to climb on myself, accidentally caught my leg in the big wheel. The driver of the wagon could not hear the frantic shouts of my friends because of the noise made by the loose plank flooring of the wagon on the dirt road. I was being pulled further and further by the spokes into the wheel. It was only when my leg was almost severed and hanging by a few ligaments that the driver finally heard the screaming of my friends, stopped the wagon and pulled me out of the wheel. They got me home somehow. The doctor wanted to amputate my leg but my mother wouldn't let him, insisting that he graft the leg onto the thigh. My youth saved the leg, which was in a cast for six months. The only permanent result of the accident is that my right leg is a little shorter than my left one.

Iron Ridge was a very little town and there was already another general store there owned by a man named Grabbow. If my mother's curses had had any efficacy whatever, Grabbow should have been dead shortly after we opened our store. We had an old-fashioned register, something like an open grate, in our sitting room above the store and mother would keep a sharp eye to the hole and count the customers in our store. Then she would look out the window and count the wagons in front of Grabbow's store, which was just across the street from our own. If Grabbow had more wagons than we did, the curses would fly. I used to wonder how the poor man could survive such inspired cursing. The register in the living room became known as "Grabbow's Hole."

We were a large family, ten children, and in spite of mother's curses, Grabbow prospered and we didn't. The little town was just unable to support two stores and we moved to Oconomowoc, Wisconsin, about the year 1909, a larger town and one which appeared to be able to support another family.

I was the baby of our family and consequently some of my oldest brothers and sisters had children who were near my own age. I was a very youthful uncle to these nieces and nephews. Next to me in age was my sister Esther, who was three years my elder. Esther was an attractive and a popular girl, but there were no Jewish boys in Oconomowoc and she was forbidden to date gentile boys. The poor girl consequently went dateless unless she could sneak one in between her watchful parents and her overzealous younger brother who hovered over his sister like a rooster hovers over his hens.

Our house in Oconomowoc was a large wooden affair with five bedrooms and one bath. It was directly on the shore of Fowler Lake, with a big yard and a barn. Our house was the second from the bridge dividing Fowler Lake into upper and lower. It was located in the part of town called Norway because many of the residents were of Norwegian descent and the Norwegian church was situated several blocks from our house. The kitchen was large and it was the room in the house where most of the activity took place. Mother never seemed to finish cooking and baking. In between there was the washing and ironing and darning and sewing, etc. Indeed her work, although aided by three teen-aged daughters who were still at home, was never done. How she managed all this work and tend a garden, keep herself tidy and a husband happy, I will never know. I never saw mother once sit down in a chair and rest. She was on her feet from six in the morning until ten at night.

Oconomowoc at this time (1909–1918) was just emerging from a sleepy resort village. It was surrounded by beautiful lakes and had become a playground for the very rich. Close to Milwaukee and Chicago the socialites built elaborate houses on these lovely lakes and lived in them with the opulence of kings. Here were the Beggs, Valentines, Montgomery Wards, etc., all situated on handsome estates. The town, for the most part, catered to its rich clientele. There was no industry except tourism. I, of course, was unaware of this; I only knew that we had settled in a most beautiful spot and I proceeded to make the most of it.

In the summer I fished and swam and hiked in the Fowler Lake area with occasional excursions into Lac La Belle, which was attached to Fowler Lake by a dam, or I would take a longer trip down the channel with my old rowboat and enter Oconomowoc Lake, gaping at the elaborate houses, some of them with their own zoos on the huge estates.

Fowler Lake at this period was clean and clear as a spring and full of fish, particularly bass, bluegills and pickerel. The banks of the lake were overhung with big willows and cottonwoods. The big bay of the lake, setting off the thirteen acres of the Binzel estate, was filled with giant water lilies, effectively preventing noisy boats from entering the bay and disturbing their peace.

We were the only Jewish family in Oconomowoc and I was called Jew by a few children but I found anti-Semitism more of a nuisance than a scourge. Besides, I was too young to understand anti-Semitism. Only once did I experience a painful fight when a bully physically attacked me. This was a child of a poor family who would ambush me on my long walk to school. It became a daily fear of running the gauntlet to escape this ruffian's taunts and finally, in desperation, I decided to fight back. We fought in the school ground just before the last bell rang. I was small for my age but what I lacked in size, I gained in swiftness and rage. I was able to dodge most of the heavy blows of my enemy and somehow received strength from I know not where. It is claimed that rage and terror lend one strength and this must be true because I threw the bully down and was on top of him pummeling unmercifully. The entire school was watching us. I did not hear the bell, and the principal had a difficult time pulling me off my adversary. We were both bloody and threatened with expulsion and my father and brother were required to come to school and explain my side of the fight.

I was not expelled and was never again threatened by the bully, and strange to report, I had actually achieved a new respect from my schoolmates. This episode had a strange climax. Many years later when I was established in my own bookstore in Milwaukee, a tall, gray-haired, rather seedy looking man appeared and inquired if I was the Harry Schwartz who had attended school in Oconomowoc. I said I was, from about 1910 to 1918. He then told me that he was the principal of the school I attended. He remembered my fight with the bully and we had a very pleasant time remembering incidents of my youth. I finally asked what he had come to see me about and he told me the following story. Some years after I had left Oconomowoc he had got himself involved with a high-school girl and was discharged. The scandal was a *cause célèbre* with the result that he was blacklisted and could not get a teaching job. The poor wretch was desperate and had written a book dealing with his experiences, which he wanted me to publish. I explained that I had no money, was not a publisher, but rather a very poor bookseller, and was genuinely sorry that I could not help him.

To return to my memories of Oconomowoc. I had an unfortunate stammer throughout my school years and it made recitation difficult for me. Frequently I would choose not to recite at all and accept a zero, although I knew the answer. My schoolmates would jeer at me and even my teachers were far from sympathetic. I enrolled in a course of public speaking hoping that this would benefit my stutter. I also began to memorize speeches and verse, believing that this would improve my speech. To this end I memorized the complete poem *Horatius* by Lord Macaulay. It so happened that I had a mean teacher for my Public Speaking class. I believed that she actually obtained pleasure in humiliating me before the students. For our final examination the class was told to memorize a speech or poem of our choice, of a minimum of twenty lines. I chose *Horatius*, of course, which I had memorized already and which I now perfected. On the day of the examination, I was called on first, which I had expected, and I announced in a clear voice that my recitation was *Horatius* by Thomas Babington Macaulay. The teacher believed that I would only recite a small part of this famous poem, probably the famous Horatius at the Bridge episode, not suspecting that I had memorized the entire poem of seventy stanzas and eight lines to a stanza or 560 lines. But I did. Moreover, I recited the entire poem without a solitary stammer and the class was jubilant because I had preempted the whole period and no one could be called upon to recite. The teacher was frustrated and angry and I had had my small revenge.

Being small in stature I did not pursue any sports and because of my speech impediment, I became somewhat of a loner. Of course, as I grew older I looked longingly at the girls, but again because of my speech difficulties I remained aloof. Because of this, some of my schoolmates believed that I was unfriendly or as they called it "stuck up." Surrounded as I was by three teen-aged sisters in the house I was frequently in a state of romantic excitement. I had a frightful inferiority complex because of my stammer and looked wistfully at my schoolgirl companions as something unattainable. They, however, attributed my shyness to the fact that I was Jewish and felt superior to them. I loved the girls, yearned for their company and grew excited merely watching them from afar.

My happiest days were spent on Fowler Lake; in the winter, skating, iceboating, skiing. I developed a trapping line and one winter trapped seventy-five muskrats, which I skinned and sold for one dollar a skin. The summers were passed fishing, boating, swimming and camping. I read voraciously, devouring all the boys' books in the public library. My life was not all play and I worked in the store after school and all day Saturday. It was my job to fill the shelves with canned goods and fill the bins with staples like coffee, sugar, flour, etc. This was before the days when everything was packaged and much of the food was sold in bulk. Remember all this preceded the automobile, chain store and supermarket. All the stores delivered their merchandise with a horse and wagon. Our horse was old and sad-looking, and for some preposterous reason we called him Caesar, hardly an appropriate name considering his appearance. It was my responsibility to feed Caesar on Saturday, Sunday and holidays. Father gave me Hebrew lessons and we read the Bible in Hebrew. Inevitably, because of my stutter, I found the Hebrew alphabet difficult to pronounce. Finally in exasperation father threw the Hebrew grammar at me, and following mother's intervention my Hebrew lessons were ended. I had just turned twelve years old and began my first fast that Yom Kippur.

I was on my way to feed Caesar when the thought suddenly struck me. I was hungry and decided to stop in the store, which was closed for the Jewish Holidays, and eat some cheese and crackers. And if there was a God, of which I was already in doubt, he could strike me dead. I was not struck down, and that was the end of my belief in God and also the end of my fasting. My closest friends were Donald Anderson and Raymond Weber, both of whom are dead, and we were frequently engaged in some harmless mischief. One of our favorite pranks was stealing apples from the orchard of the Binzel estate. The Binzels were wealthy brewers who lived on thirteen acres on Fowler Lake just north of us. The grounds were surrounded by a stone wall, which we climbed, and filling our shirts with apples, scrambled back over the wall.

Sometimes, before we reached the safety of the other side of the wall, we were shot at. This puzzled us because we were certain that there was nobody around to observe us. The house was situated far back near the lake and we couldn't understand how anyone could detect us in the orchard.

This was a mystery we never did solve until many years later. In the meantime the Binzels all died and the estate was willed to the city of Oconomowoc for a park in their memory. I would make a pilgrimage to Oconomowoc yearly, look at the house we lived in, at the building that housed our general store and drive up to the Binzel park now owned by the city. The stone fence was demolished but their old house survived. Vandals had broken some windows and these were boarded up.

One year while picnicking in the Binzel Park I noticed a park employee enter the old boarded-up house. Curious, I followed him and asked him if I could look in the house, which was empty and deserted. Of course I told him who I was and recalled to him my experiences when a boy in the apple orchard. He listened to my story and said, "Of course I know you, I'm _____ and we used to steal cookies from your father's store." In the house I noticed a tall ladder which led up to the roof of the house. I climbed the ladder to a sort of parapet from which could be observed the entire surrounding countryside, and the puzzle of the Binzel orchard was solved. Binzel, standing on the parapet with binoculars, watched us kids stealing his apples and shot at us mainly for the fun of observing us run. One year later the house was demolished, so I had got into it and found the ladder and parapet just in time. And today the good townspeople of Oconomowoc flock to the Binzel Park on weekends, little knowing that only sixty years ago little boys stole apples right where they are now barbecuing their bratwurst.

CHAPTER II

During the years 1922, 1923 and part of the year 1924 I had hitchhiked back and forth across America. Hitchhiking at this time was a necessity and not something you did in protest against something, as is done today. You simply hitchhiked because you had no automobile and no money. Today it is an accepted mode of travel and even well-to-do people use their thumbs to hitch a ride. Most of these trips were uneventful and the result of boredom and restlessness. However, one of these journeys, my first to the West Coast, is worthwhile recording in some detail.

In the summer of 1923 Sam Pessin suggested that we buy an old car and leisurely motor to the West Coast. I became acquainted with Sam, who was considerably older than I, due to his brother having married one of my sisters. He was a brilliant fellow, striking in appearance, although not particularly attractive. He had a swarthy complexion, aquiline nose and piercing black eyes. Women were attracted to him and he had quantities of what is sometimes called sex appeal. He was also remarkably articulate and had great powers of persuasion. Sam was what one might term a literary con man. He edited and published *The Milwaukee Arts Monthly* for its brief span of life—three numbers from Milwaukee and two from Chicago, where it changed its name to *Prairie*. It was almost certain, although I was too naive to be aware of it, that Sam was compelled to flee the city to escape his creditors.

As neither of us knew anything about the mechanics of an automobile, I suggested that we enlist somebody to go with us who did. I recommended Elmer Kaliebe, one of my high school acquaintances with whom I had become friendly, and who worked part time at Caspar's Bookstore. You will hear more of this old bookstore in these memoirs.

We pooled together one hundred dollars each, of which we spent one hundred and fifty dollars for a 1916 Maxwell. This was supposed to be a camping trip so we bought a tent, folding cots, cooking utensils, etc., etc.

It is difficult to describe the pleasures of traveling along the highways during this period. It was not only the absence of the expressways, the scourge of present-day motor travel, but the lack of hordes of impatient motorists. It was a grasping of adventure, of fresh air, unpolluted streams. This was long before the era of camping grounds or the explosion of camping parks, and before the highways were congested with campers all heading for the parks and camping sites. Instead of billboards there were wide open spaces; in place of endless ribbons of concrete there were woods and browsing cattle and horses, pigs, sheep and poultry. The landscape was beautiful and driving was a pleasure.

We were up at dawn and camped wherever we pleased. We would usually pull up beside a stream, pitch our tent and prepare our food before a fire. Everything went according to plan until we approached Miles City, Montana, where we met with an accident.

The elevation had begun to ascend rapidly and in some areas gave way to sizable foothills, for we had begun the long climb of the Rocky Mountains. Unfortunately, Sam was driving one morning as we wound up a steep road and instead of throwing the gear into low for a climb of this grade, he kept the gear in high, stalled the motor and frantically pulled the hand brake as the car began to pick up speed backwards downhill. It was at this moment that we discovered that the brakes did not hold. Both sides of the road had steep inclines—one was a sharp precipice-like drop, while the other, although steep, was yet manageable. Through luck, which had nothing to do with steering, the car chose the lesser of the two inclines, and came to a complete stop at the bottom, with all three of us sitting upright as if frozen to our seats. Sam and I had our hands glued to the hand brake, which acted liked a seat belt and prevented us from being thrown out of the automobile. Elmer was squeezed in like an anchovy among the camping paraphernalia in the back seat. When we recovered our senses after a few minutes and examined the car, we found all four wheels snapped off as cleanly as though cut with a knife. But more devastating, the engine was cracked right down the middle, which Elmer discovered by crawling underneath the car.

Following the shock of the accident we held a strategy conference. What to do now? We had spent very little money except for gasoline and oil thus far, so that our original nest egg was almost intact. Should we attempt to have the car repaired and continue, or should we try to sell it and hitchhike? Repairing the car would unquestionably require a long delay and very likely be expensive. We decided to sell the car and agreed that Elmer should do all the talking as he was the only one of us who knew anything about automobiles.

Miles City, Montana, at this time was a small city (present population 7,313) known primarily as a leading cattle town of the region. To celebrate the Fourth of July, the city became famous for a rodeo that operated for three days, July 4, 5, and 6.

It was our luck to be stranded in this town during the Rodeo. We sought out a garage that was open and Elmer told the proprietor our story. The owner of the garage drove us out to look at the wreck. He examined the axles and the wheels, looked under the hood and shook his head. "I can't repair this old junker," he said. "I haven't any wheels that will fit it. I'll have to send away for wheels and that will take at least six weeks." When we heard this our spirits sank. How could we possibly spend six weeks in Miles City waiting for wheels? Elmer suggested that the mechanic buy the car. "Naw," he said, "I don't need another car." Elmer reminded him that after the car was repaired he could sell it for a fat profit because the car was in perfect condition except for the wheels.

Elmer noticed that the mechanic was attracted to our camping equipment and offered to throw in all the equipment if he would buy the automobile. That did it and we got an offer of $100 for the car and all our goods. We drove back to the garage and were given a check which Elmer refused to accept because we had no way of cashing it. We were unknown at the bank, complete strangers in town and how could we possibly cash a hundred-dollar check? Moreover, suppose the check was worthless or suppose he stopped payment on it. Following considerable discussion the owner of the garage agreed to accompany us to the bank and vouch for us. We cashed the check, registered at the hotel and only then allowed ourselves the luxury of congratulating each other. But we had escaped from an extremely rotten situation only to stumble into an even worse one.

We had been fortunate in arriving in Miles City on the third of July because, as mentioned earlier, the Rodeo in celebration of the Fourth of July continued for three days and, of course, everything in town would be closed down. We watched the Rodeo for a time but the events of riding broncos, steers, calves, and the dexterity with the lasso began to bore us. Elmer, an excellent dancer, besides being a handsome fellow, lost little time in attracting a girl, of which there appeared to be an abundance to choose from. The town was jumping and the sun was broiling. Sam and I decided to seek other diversion. We had little difficulty in locating a speakeasy, for remember this was during prohibition, and discovered a pretty good beer. After consuming several bottles we were about to return to our hotel when we were accosted by two strangers. What follows will remind you of a script for a present-day western. Moreover, it is a script which is so threadbare that it is difficult to believe that it actually happened to us in 1923, and not in 1870.

The two strangers confessed that they were bored, as we were, and suggested a "little action." Sam and I, feeling a pleasant glow from the beer and remembering that we had a fat wallet, agreed. The marvel is that both Sam and I, who had read stories of cardsharpers from Bret Harte to Mark Twain, did not have our suspicions aroused. Neither of us suspected these strangers were other than what they professed to be: bored businessmen looking for a friendly game. One of the men proposed his room at the hotel, where we were also staying, and we accepted gladly. The game was to be five-card draw poker, jacks or better to open. Five-dollar limit was suggested and agreed to.

For the first several hours the game was pleasant and we were about even. I should interpolate here that both Sam and I were excellent poker players. I had played with my father and brothers for small stakes all through my high-school years. Sam had played for years for much larger stakes, so we were not exactly neophytes. Elmer was still dancing with his young lady and it was nearing midnight. We had been winning a small amount and one of the men suggested that we raise the limit. We all agreed to a no-limit contest. It was at this point that the action jumped. Sam, who had two pair aces up, opened for five dollars. The stranger next to him stayed. I was going for an inside straight but decided that even if I connected, I would not win, and dropped out. But before discarding my cards I had studied them carefully. I remembered discarding a ten of clubs among my five cards. The dealer, who I had grown to dislike because he made me uneasy, raised the pot fifty dollars. Sam stayed and the next man dropped his cards. Sam drew one card and connected with aces full. To non-poker players I might explain that this is one of the best hands a player can hold. The dealer drew two cards. Sam bet fifty dollars. He did it so casually that one would think he was a professional gambler. I, on the other hand, was a wreck. My heart was pounding and I was mentally calculating how much money we had. The dealer called Sam's fifty and raised one hundred. I suspected we were in trouble. Sam asked to have the game suspended and told me to go to our room and bring the remainder of our money. There was one hundred dollars in ten-dollar bills and a few dollars in change.

Sam called the bet and showed his aces full. He began to reach for the pot but the dealer displayed four tens. Of course four of a kind beats a full house; however, I spotted the ten of clubs among the four the dealer showed and shouted out that there was something crooked about the hand. How could there be five tens in one deck of cards? Frantically I began searching for the ten of clubs that I had discarded, but at this point the dealer drew a gun and, pointing it at me, intimated that it would not be healthy for me to cause any trouble. He scooped up all the money on the table and, frightened, we made our exit as quickly as we could.

We were thoroughly intimidated and were trembling with fear. When we recovered we thought of notifying the police or the hotel management, but decided against it for it might get us into even deeper trouble. It was a classic example of cardsharping and we were the perfect dupes. We were stranded without any money, no car, no equipment and now we owed a hotel bill. At this point Elmer returned and from our appearance he suspected that something terrible had occurred. We told him the story and were worried that he would scold us for gambling with his share of the money. Instead of being angry with us, he blamed himself for having been extravagant and spent all the money he had on him.

Our next problem was how to escape from the hotel without paying for our room. It was now the Fourth of July and the Rodeo was going full blast. The town was crowded with cowboys and girls. The hotel was jammed. We had noticed that when the clerk of the hotel was busy looking for a key, checking for mail, or otherwise engaged, it was easy for anyone to slip out of the hotel lobby without being observed. Therefore, we decided that Sam should detain the clerk and Elmer and I should make our escape with our two bags which contained everything the three of us owned. Sam would follow us later. We had learned that a freight train was due at about 8:30 that evening. It slowed down to drop off the mail and went on to Butte, Montana. We decided to catch this train if we could. Elmer and I succeeded in getting out of the hotel unseen while Sam kept the clerk occupied and blocked his vision. No bellhops were in sight.

We arrived in Butte early in the morning and as we crouched in our boxcar and stared out at the wild landscape, the mountains covered with forests, a thrill surged through us, for this was our first view of the real American West. It was also my first experience riding in an empty boxcar and I enjoyed it. We counted our money and found we had a total of seven dollars, all that remained after our fleecing by the

cardsharpers. We registered at the Tait Hotel, a cheap, run-
down hostelry, and immediately began looking for work.
Butte was the largest city in Montana at this time, and when
Marcus Daly founded the Anaconda Copper Co. and began to
exploit "the richest hill on earth" it was a wide open town. We
first made the rounds of the employment offices, where they
scribbled the available jobs in chalk on long blackboards. All
these offers for work were for manual labor, and Sam and
Elmer had little difficulty in securing employment, Sam in a
potato field and Elmer, who was a husky six-footer, as a farm
laborer. I, a little shrimp, whose weight was about 120 pounds,
was rejected.

Being unsuccessful in obtaining farm work I studied the
want ads in the newspaper and found a job selling the Harvard
Classics. This, as everyone knows, is a set of books of fifty
volumes containing many of the great works of mankind. The
job appealed to me primarily because it paid two dollars a day
and I was given a free sample. We were divided into crews of
four or five men, and each crew had a captain whose job it
was to observe that we actually rang doorbells and tried to sell
books instead of goofing off. The selling procedure was
typical of all house-to-house selling, mainly to surprise the
occupant, overwhelm her with false promises and get a deposit
(our salary) and a signature on a contract that she, of course,
did not read. And there was always the inducement of free
magazines, dictionaries, atlases, etc.

We were an uninspired gang of hucksters and one week on
the job was all that I could tolerate. The captain of our crew
was an aggressive ignoramus who drove us like cattle to
perform his canvassing.

I still have the letters that Sam addressed to me at the Tait
Hotel. He now used the name William Falk. One letter was
postmarked July 17, 1923 and was addressed to Harry

Kingston, a fancy name that I assumed, another being Camille Vincennes. Sam also used the name Gregory Geonodorff and, of course, his pen name was Lawrence Drake, under which he wrote what appeared to be his only book, *Dont Call Me Clever*, published by Simon & Schuster in 1929. Elmer chucked his haymaking job at the same time that I quit and together we jumped on a freight train heading for Cody, Wyoming. Cody was a little town in northwestern Wyoming on the Shoshone River and was a cattle market and also a tourist center for Yellowstone National Park, for which we were bound. Named for Colonel William F. Cody (Buffalo Bill) the town had a museum and celebrated Buffalo Bill's birthday. Our empty boxcar proved to be excellent for sightseeing and we could not have chosen a better method to observe the countryside. The landscape was wild and the timber was virgin forest. There were few towns along the railroad and absolutely nothing to spoil the view. Scores of wildflowers and plants grew everywhere in profusion. Wild game was in abundance and we observed an occasional deer staring at us. We hitchhiked to Mammoth Hot Springs Hotel and, of course, our first concern was to find work. We had not yet become bums and preferred to pay for our food and lodging. The same difficulty plagued me here as in Butte. The management hired Elmer immediately but took one look at me and motioned me away. I had begun to suspect a subtle form of anti-Semitism was at work in spite of the French name, Camille Vincennes, which I had now taken.

I had little trouble finding food. I would simply sneak into the kitchen with Elmer and pretend I was an employee. But locating a place to sleep presented a problem. The kitchen help bunked in long rows of dormitories in the rear of the hotel, but there were no extra bunks and it appeared that I would be compelled to sleep outdoors. Although this was August the temperature fell rapidly after sunset and the nights became chilly. The prospect of spending the night outdoors did not appeal to me, particularly as I had no blanket, coat or other covering. Then I learned, through one of the employees, that one bedroom on the ground floor of the hotel was usually vacant. The room was held in reserve by the management and apparently used only in an emergency. I was advised to wait until nightfall, then steal into the room and without switching on the lights, crawl into bed. I was warned to get out of the room before daylight. I followed instructions and entered the room, with some misgivings, without being seen, and without switching on the electric lights, I crawled into bed. I stretched out, luxuriating in the belief that I was about to enjoy a good night's sleep. Suddenly, I became paralyzed with fright; my foot had touched another foot in the bed and it wasn't mine. I lay breathless, not knowing what to do. Should I shout out or run from the room? The foot had retreated after I touched it so I knew it was not a dead body. While I was considering what to do the door opened and another body crawled into bed. I then realized that I was not the only one who knew about the spare room and it was apparently a night lodging for any unfortunate who did not have a bed.

I slept in this bed for a week without knowing who my bed companions were and I continued as an uninvited guest in the kitchen eating at the hotel's expense. Elmer and I had arranged beforehand that, should I get caught, I should head for West Yellowstone, the western edge of the park and wait for him. This is precisely what happened. One day as I was eating breakfast in the kitchen I noticed two men who I had not seen before watching me. I knew immediately I was suspected. They continued to keep me under surveillance for awhile and one of them walked over to me and asked me quietly to follow him to his office. In his office he asked me to sit down and he began the following interrogation.

"What is your name?"

"Camille Vincennes," I told him.

"Why are you eating in the kitchen although you are not working for the hotel?"

"Because, although I have tried repeatedly to get a job I have been unable to do so, and ate in the kitchen because I was hungry."

"Did you not know that you are eating food for which you are not paying?"

"Yes, I know it, but what does one do when one is hungry and has no money and cannot find work," I asked.

"Well you owe the hotel for one week's food and if you have no money I will have to arrest you."

When I heard the word "arrest" I bolted for the open door and reaching it, I flew down a driveway to a road leading out of the Park. Fortunately an old truck was crawling along the highway heaped with camping equipment. I jumped in and covered up. My good luck held and I learned that the truck was headed for West Yellowstone, the western edge of the Park. Here, as arranged, I met Elmer. It seems that the hotel people had attempted to hold him responsible for my food (they did not know of the hotel bedroom), but he denied that he knew me so vigorously that he succeeded in convincing them.

We crossed the Continental Divide and via freight train and hitchhiking decided that Salt Lake City would be our next destination. We sped through Idaho Falls on a freight train and hitchhiked and walked through Pocatello, where we observed stud poker being played on the sidewalks right out in the open. We lived very frugally, subsisting for the most part on milk, cheese and bread. There was fruit for the picking, particularly grapes, peaches and pears. We slept outdoors in the fields or woods. One night we missed a freight train and fell asleep in the tiny depot where we were arrested for vagrancy. However, we were not detained long and quickly got out of that town. In spite of our minimum diet and exposure we were quite healthy until we arrived in Salt Lake City, where Elmer became ill. It was ironic that he, a six-footer weighing over 200 pounds, should have succumbed rather than I, who now weighed about half as much. We rented a room in a cheap hotel and Elmer crawled into bed. I brought him aspirin and oranges and following two days of rest he recovered. The only work I was able to find was shining shoes and Elmer obtained a job in a meat market, slicing the accumulated fat off the walls of a cooler.

Unfortunately at this period in my life I was less concerned with observing the beauty or ugliness of cities than I was with self-preservation. I was usually so close to hunger that I was mostly concerned with our minimal needs and gave little thought to the beauty of things. As a consequence, Salt Lake City—which I understand is a beautiful city—at the time I was a shoeshine boy in it, did not appear beautiful at all. To me it was only a big Mormon city with exceptionally wide streets that required a long time to cross.

I attended memorial services for President Harding at the Mormon Tabernacle, not knowing then about his clandestine entanglement. The notorious book *The President's Daughter*, alleging that Harding had been conducting an illicit love affair and had sired an illegitimate child, was not published for several years. (*The President's Daughter* was published by the Elizabeth Ann Guild in 1927 and enjoyed a large, if underground sale.) The famous Teapot Dome scandals were to burst later.

Our next destination was Los Angeles and, with the exception of being thrown into jail in Las Vegas because we were riding a freight train, there is little that is worth recording. Las Vegas originally was a watering place for the wagon trains en route to southern California. Several forts were built and eventually it became a shipping center for cattle and sheep and a farm region. Of course this was long before Las Vegas became a tourist trap and a gambling haven. At this time it was a sleepy little mining and cattle town and did not even dream of its future notoriety. We were incarcerated for only a brief period in an outdoor tin lockup and were warned that railroads were private property and to stay off. We succeeded in finding work in a restaurant that had two distinctions; it was cheap and served hardly anything except pork. I previously had not realized that the pig was as useful to the white man as the buffalo was to the Indian. Our restaurant served a form of pork every day and little else. It served roast pork, pork chops, pork pie, spare ribs, pork sausage, pickled pigs feet and, of course, ham, bacon and lard. When we quit our jobs we were so saturated with pork that to this day, fifty years later, the mere thought of eating pork nauseates me.

As a farewell present the owner of the restaurant packed a bag of pork sandwiches which we promptly gave to the first hitchhiker we met. The money we earned in the restaurant restored our confidence and we leisurely reached Los Angeles in the evening atop a freight train and narrowly escaped arrest again. We learned later that the Southern Pacific Railroad was particularly angry because tramps broke the seals on freight cars and goods had been stolen. As a consequence railroad detectives cracked down on all riders of freight cars, even empty ones, and more detectives, or railroad bulls as we called them, began patrolling all freight trains. It was during this period of extra patrols that we were detected on a freight in the middle of the Mojave Desert and thrown off the train as it slowed down. Elmer and I endured one of the most frightful nights of our entire trip and nearly froze to death. The Mojave Desert gets very cold and an intense rainstorm added to our misery.

Los Angeles had not yet become the sprawling polluted metropolis it was to grow into. At this time it was beautiful, uncrowded and clean. We spent several weeks exploring the city, taking advantage of all the free rides and lunches the real estate touts offered. The city was in the throes of a real estate boom and prospects were cajoled with free lunches and suppers and a bus ride to its holdings. I attempted a job at Central Casting but was passed by. We invariably ate at a cafeteria called The Pioneer Lunch, where everything was priced in units of seven cents. A sandwich cost seven cents; ham and eggs cost fourteen cents; soup, seven cents a bowl, etc. For about twenty-eight cents with judicious selection we got a pretty good meal.

Our money was nearly exhausted again and I secured a job in a secondhand bookstore on Sixth Street in downtown Los Angeles. Sixth Street was lined with bookstores, many of them secondhand, and although it was not a Fourth Avenue in New York, it was the largest aggregation of bookstores I had ever seen. Although I knew little about books at this time, maybe this was the seed that was to grow into the bookman I was to become. At this time it was only a job, but books were to become a passion. On one of my walks I was amazed to find a canyon filled to overflowing with oranges. This struck me as strange indeed, because oranges were selling in stores at five cents each; and, of course, this was the famous orange country. I had not yet heard of the criminal dumping and ploughing under of food to maintain its price through artificial shortages.

What was responsible for the idea that I return to school escapes me; however, I did return to Milwaukee and entered

Normal School, which was the predecessor of the present University of Wisconsin, Milwaukee. My enthusiasm for formal education did not last long, and in the fall of 1924, I was off on another "excursion," this time to the East Coast and New York, where I found a job in the insurance business. Though the insurance business is the last occupation I would have chosen to enter, in this case I had little choice. Jobs were not easy to obtain in New York and I had no skills. Moreover the economy was experiencing a recession, a well-known phenomenon in capitalist economy. My brother Isadore had found a job with the Metropolitan Life Insurance Co. in New York, and with the help of my brother I obtained a similar position with the John Hancock Life Insurance Co.

My work consisted of collecting nickels and dimes from families once a week. Usually a family with two or more children had a small policy on each family member, and sometimes both father and mother had three, four or more policies. As a consequence many homes were forced to pay premiums from one to six dollars a week. Agents were habitually unscrupulous and loaded a family beyond its ability to make payments. The result was that policies inevitably lapsed and the poor families not only lost their money but lost their insurance too. Of course, this was before legislation was passed correcting some of the worst abuses. But in the period of which I am writing [1925–1926] it was possible for a dishonest insurance agent to exploit the poor people on his debit to the hilt. My debit extended from 167th to 173rd Streets along Third Avenue, a shabby neighborhood under the elevated. It was not long before I became outraged at what transpired around me and I attempted to quit. My manager, a shrewd, short, potbellied fellow refused to let me go. He had been in the Industrial Insurance business a long time, and he knew, he said, how youngsters first reacted to this jungle behavior; he explained patiently that I would regard all this tolerantly in a short time. My brother also tried to convince me that "this was the system" and one had to accept it. After the first period of revulsion had passed, I tried to accommodate my conscience. I reasoned that if I did not collect these premiums from the "poor devils" somebody else, more ruthless than I, would. But the real circumstance that was responsible for my continuing on the job, and which numbed my conscience, was the fact that I was earning a good deal of money for the first time in my life and enjoyed spending it. How easy it is to "accommodate one's conscience" was graphically illustrated to me by this job. Money, of course, was the villain. Pay a man enough money and he will do most anything. That is one reason why certain jobs that require considerable "accommodation of conscience" pay quite well. Strike-breaking is a good example.

Of all the numerous places that New York offers to spend one's time and money, it was the bookshops that mainly attracted me. I believe that this was the first time that I began thinking of bookselling as a career. I observed the small cozy stores usually with only one, sometimes two, people in attendance. There was no dishonesty or sharpness in this business, or so I thought, and quite a contrast to my present occupation.

I hurried to complete my duties on the debit so I could "take off" for the bookshops. On my day off I usually took the subway to Fourth Avenue, which was, at that time, the hub of the secondhand book business, and starting at one end I made the rounds of as many stores as possible before closing time. I spent hour after hour browsing in the dusty stores. Frequently I would forget to have lunch, not for lack of money, but because I was too engrossed to notice that I was hungry. I was especially infatuated by the five- and ten-cent bins. And the day I found a copy in a ten-cent bin, albeit soiled and worn, of the *Anatomy of Tobacco*, because the proprietor (perhaps) did not know it was by Arthur Machen, I was very happy indeed.

New York, at this time, had an extensive assortment of bookshops. There were swanky establishments uptown, the numerous neighborhood gift and card shops that also sold books, and my special joy, the myriads of secondhand bookshops. Fourth Avenue was the book buyer's paradise then, but there were bookshops all over the city. There were bookshops in Harlem, in the Village, Uptown, Downtown, Eastside, Westside, everywhere. Even under the sidewalks. One day I was walking on Second Avenue, when I noticed a grimy fellow descend into a cellar under the sidewalk with an armful of books. I waited a few minutes and he reappeared, collected another armful from a push-cart, and was about to descend again, when I asked him if the books were for sale. He said they were and motioned me to follow him into his crypt. There were thousands of books in that basement but it was difficult to examine them. The old bookman was a scout who sold primarily to dealers. He spent his days picking over the junk in old furniture stores, warehouses, auctions, etc., and bought what seemed salable. What he didn't sell immediately he stored in his cellar.

Some days I exchanged the milieu of Fourth Avenue for the swank uptown shops. Browsing among the shelves of the Brick Row Bookshop, which at this time was located at 19 East 47th Street (they have since moved to Austin, Texas), was always a remarkable experience. However, these were books for the rich and were not intended for mere insurance agents. There were first editions of Shelley and Keats and, of course, such celebrated classics as Boswell's Johnson, etc. Another uptown shop that attracted me was Edgar H. Wells, who at this time was at 602 Madison Avenue. Wells had a fascinating stock of books mostly in impeccable condition and, although I knew that I could afford none of these rarities, it was a pleasure merely to look at them and read the titles. Of course, much later I did acquire the kind of library that only a rich man is supposed to own. My Faulkner collection of first editions was recently sold at the Parke-Bernet Galleries and brought a very large sum. Shortly after I sold my Faulkner collection my wife and I were having breakfast in a restaurant on Madison Avenue in New York. I happened to look up across the street and noticed the Philip Duschnes bookshop on the second floor. I had sold Duschnes many books including lots of Faulkner first editions and received his excellent catalogs.

On entering his store we were greeted by Phil, who immediately brought his wife out of the office and introduced us as follows: "Darling this is Mr. and Mrs. Schwartz from Milwaukee. He's the fellow who cornered the market on Faulkner first editions, having bought them at 39 cents and is now unloading them with a heavy profit." Looking over his stock I found many of my books which he had bought at my Faulkner sale at the Parke-Bernet. His remark that I had bought my Faulkners for 39 cents a copy referred to my having bought one hundred copies of *Go Down Moses* at 60 cents each and sold many of them for sums up to fifty dollars. My copy brought fifty-five dollars at the Parke-Bernet sale.

Another shop I frequently visited was that of L. Weitz at 439 Madison Avenue. This store specialized in fine bindings, which always made me think of furniture and not books. Later I learned that a fine binding on a good book can be a beautiful adjunct to anybody's library. But a library consisting of fine bindings alone still causes me to associate it with furniture.

I still knew comparatively little about books but I studied every catalog I was able to obtain. There has been too little written about catalogs. They are the classrooms and textbooks of the antiquarian book trade. Without them it would be infinitely more difficult to learn about books, particularly bibliography. A huge amount of book knowledge goes into each catalog, and the anonymous catalogers who compile these diminutive pamphlets are frequently scholars. I learned that a book can be extremely rare, but not worth very much. Rarity, I learned, is not synonymous with expensive. Books are not collected or valued because of rarity alone. However, once a given book is desirable for various reasons such as intrinsic importance, it does become more valuable depending on how scarce or rare it is. When I moved to downtown Milwaukee from Downer Avenue in 1937, in the mistaken belief that I would no longer need them I sold 500 catalogs. This was one of the many mistakes I made and one that I have never ceased to regret. Fortunately I did save long runs of what I considered indispensable catalogs. Although my catalogs still number in the hundreds I will mention only a few here. The catalogs of George Bates, a London bookseller who may no longer be in business, were remarkable, containing extraordinary books. The catalogs of Elkin Mathews Ltd., the firm of London booksellers that Percy Muir was associated with (see *Minding My Own Business*, London, 1956), were always interesting and informative. My catalogs of Bertram Rota start with number 65 issued in 1940 and today number almost two hundred. Rota's catalogs are among the best in the first-edition business. They do not abound in great rarities and the prices are modest, but the selection is large and there are many out-of-the-way items that you seldom spot in catalogs. Bibliographically they are accurate and when a book is cataloged as in good condition it is generally a little better than good.

My catalogs even fulfilled a purpose for which they were not intended—a prop for a television show. When I read that delightful memoir "84 Charing Cross Road" by Helen Hanff, I remembered that I had some of this bookseller's catalogs in my possession. I wrote her asking if she would like them, of course, without charge. Her letter to me dated March 16, 1971 follows:

"Dear Mr. Schwartz, Can't tell you what you'll be doing for me when those catalogues get here. It's not just that I don't have a single one to remember Marks & Co. by; its that "84 c c r" is to be done by Net next season (over the Los Angeles station but to be shown nationwide on the Educational Network) and I need a catalogue for a couple of scenes and didn't know where—or if—I'd find one. Many thanks for taking the trouble to send them. Yours Helene Hanff."

I might have remained in New York at my insurance job indefinitely but for some strange need that kept thrusting itself at me. Besides, I was unhappy selling insurance. True, I was earning a good and steady salary. But the debit or route had become an unpleasant chore, and finally it grew hateful to me. My associates in the office thought I was some kind of queer bird, and so I must have been to them. I read voraciously and brought stacks of books to the office. My desk was piled with books. The other salesmen had little sympathy for my interest in books. To them it appeared like some sort of aberration. Finally, my manager asked me not to bring books into the office. He was worried, he said, that it might detract from the work habits of his agents.

The truth is that, at this period, 1925–1926, Industrial Life Insurance was a predatory business. Its ethics were those of the jungle. Salesmen who you believed were your friends and worked at a desk beside you were surreptitiously plotting how to cheat you. Petty larceny, corruption and plain crookedness were rampant. The poor people who were sold insurance very often did not understand what they were paying for. Many of them were foreigners who could not read English. They were threatened and cheated. Pictures of destitute families unable to bury a dying child were flung at them if they hesitated to insure a newborn baby. The trick was to play on their emotions. These miserable paupers who were only one step ahead of starvation were fertile material. Some of these agents had grown so adept at frightening these people that their services were at a premium. They accompanied less successful agents on the daily rounds of debits. And through coercion and cajolery many insurance policies were put on the books.

All sorts of dodges and ruses were used to extract premiums and there were even instances of forged signatures. As a consequence many who were attracted to this work were already unscrupulous or shortly became so. Money was the only consideration; how much new business was brought in was the only yardstick. No questions were asked, and no one cared how you obtained the business or who you hurt by writing it.

For the second time I demanded of Clark, my manager, that I be allowed to resign. Clark now realized that I would never make a good insurance salesman and asked me to continue only until he found someone to replace me. This was not as easy as it appeared. Insurance companies, at that time, closed their eyes to many dishonest methods in obtaining premiums, but they were extremely careful about who they employed. Embezzlement was not uncommon. It was tempting and easy because you always carried a sizable amount of the company's money on your person. You settled your account once a week and you invariably walked around with several hundred dollars not belonging to you. It apparently was legitimate to extort premiums from underpaid janitors, but you must not touch one penny of the company's money. Finally, after six weeks, I was replaced. I had become worried that I would succumb to the life of "easy money" and all that it implied. I felt certain that had I remained another year it would have become more difficult to resign. I think that Clark knew this and that is why he refused to release me the first time I asked to resign. The shrewd old manager knew that the longer I remained with the company the less likelihood there was of my leaving. I did not have to look far to see how insidiously this life could take possession of one. My brother, Isadore, when starting with Metropolitan Life a few years before, had planned to take the job for a brief period only until something better would turn up. He, too, hated the Industrial Insurance business as it was conducted at this time. But all his hopes came to naught, and he died with the Metropolitan, caught in the fatal trap of "easy money."

I alternated my book hunting with chess playing. I had become fascinated with chess and played the game at every opportunity. At first I was a mediocre novice, but if you are any good at all you get better by playing, and eventually I became rather good. Many days, instead of working on my debit, found me playing chess in some bookshop or other.

I also played at the Stuyvesant Chess Club, but there I played for money. It was the only time I gambled with chess as, of course, there are chess hustlers as there are pool hustlers. At the club I played with a motley assortment of freaks. I remember particularly one fellow who, each time he made a move, banged his leaded chessman down on the table as if each move was chessmate. Of course by this he meant to intimidate you.

Being free of the insurance job gave me more time for book browsing, chess playing and New York Public Library reading. The Library became my university and I attended this school almost daily, reading the books I had noted in my browsing. I maintained a list of books I intended to read and continued adding to this list regularly. Occasionally I encountered an odious form of censorship. One day I asked a librarian at the Public Library for Havelock Ellis' *Studies in the Psychology of Sex*, a book that I had noted in my reading. I was told that it was a restricted book and could only be read with an attendant in the room. I objected to this but was told that this was the only way I could read the book. When I was finally handed the book, I was compelled to sit in a cubicle while an attendant observed me, hardly conducive to an enjoyable reading of Havelock Ellis.

I don't want to leave the impression that I spent all my time either working or looking for books. I prowled the city like a cat, sniffing in the most out-of-the-way places. I lived in a tiny room in Harlem and took my meals wherever I happened to be when I was hungry. There was a small cellar restaurant on Fifth Avenue that I visited at least once a week. The food was excellent and inexpensive. Many of these small restaurants specialized in only one or two dishes and they were proud of their specialties. Some took extraordinary pains with their gefilte fish; others served a most delicious herring and sour cream; and still others made fantastic potato pancakes. Yet others developed amazing soups. Of course, there were common dishes obtainable in hundreds of restaurants, but the fact is that in these little dining rooms these ordinary dishes became extraordinary, and once you had tasted knishes in one of these you would not soon forget that restaurant. In these tiny eating places without neon signs or fancy interiors the customer came only because of the food. They never advertised and many had no names, but once a customer stumbled onto the place he returned for more. These places seldom presented a menu. The waiter knew his customers and served exactly what was wanted. Many of these marvels of private enterprise were exclusively family affairs. The mother cooked, the father was majordomo and waiter, and the children, if grown, helped in the kitchen. Frequently a daughter and son waited on tables also, and the father sat up front at an improvised cashier counter reading the evening paper and observing his customers.

I had saved a little money from my insurance stint and began thinking seriously of bookselling as a career. My wanderings, which had led me to Los Angeles and New York and then to Chicago and back to New York again, always brought me back home to Milwaukee. It seemed that I was trying desperately to escape from Milwaukee, and yet, like a magnet, it always pulled me back. On one of my trips to Chicago I obtained a job at Kroch's Book Store and became, for the first time, a professional seller of new books. While working in Chicago I had met Ward Moore, who was employed in the book department of a large department store. Ward lived in a basement room in a dilapidated building on Ohio Street, and invited me to share the room with him. This was the dirtiest room I have ever lived in. However, it was only three dollars a week, big and warm. To get to it one had to navigate through a furnace area, a coal cellar, a storage room and various obstacles and smells. Ward had an excellent library, which was one of the reasons which led me to share his room. He had a complete set of George Bernard Shaw, quite a feat for this time, and sets of the important French authors, especially Flaubert and Balzac; and numerous Russian writers. It was a collection that might have distinguished a palatial residence, and looked incongruous in the cellar.

Ward and I discussed books hour after hour, and although his opinions were inflexible, we seldom quarreled. One day Ward suggested that we open a bookshop in partnership and stock it with our personal libraries. My books were now in Milwaukee, and while not as numerous as Ward's, I did have some nice editions. After nights of discussion and planning I went to Milwaukee and packed my books. Meanwhile Ward rented another basement room and we opened the Catacomb Bookshop on Indiana Street.

The idea was that Ward should continue to work and I should quit my job and manage the bookstore. We had a sign painted, built some shelves, unpacked our books, and thought we were in business. The shop was a failure from the moment it opened. We had no money for advertising and we had no customers. Ward was supposed to boost the shop among his customers at the department store, and our friends were prodded to talk it up everywhere. However, our only customers were the poor Hungarian carpenter who had built our shelves and selected books in payment and a motley collection of penniless eccentrics.

Although it was inevitable that the Catacomb Bookshop would end in failure I did not believe that it would collapse so suddenly. I was called home to Milwaukee by my mother's illness and, returning in several days, found the bookshop locked, all the books gone, and no sign of Ward anywhere. I will skip several unpleasant episodes that revolved around Ward after I retrieved my books. Of course Ward was not entirely responsible for his freakish behavior. The fellow had an abominable background. An only child, his parents were divorced while he was quite young and he was reared by his mother. Apparently there was enough money to live in comfort and although Ward's mother was still young she did not remarry. She surrounded herself with a group of intellectuals and Ward had become accustomed to a permissive and Bohemian existence.

PART TWO

Adventures in Bookselling, 1927–1972

CHAPTER III

When we are collecting books,
we are collecting happiness.

VINCENT A. STARRETT

I was introduced to Paul Romaine in 1922 when he was a
member of the Wisconsin Players, a small theatrical
group. My first impression of Paul was not conducive to
forming a partnership or opening a bookshop with him. However, it was another instance where a first impression was
totally misleading, as he did become my partner and we did
open a bookshop together; moreover, a partnership that was
only terminated by the intervention of the great depression,
and nothing resembling the hopeless Catacomb Bookshop in
Chicago. He appeared to me at this time (1922) to be a
stereotype of Henri Murger's Bohemia. He wore a velvet
jacket, shirts with low collars and neckties with enormous
loose knots. He wore his hair long and grew a neat mustache.
Of course this was fifty years before the present craze for long
hair and beards. I was not intimate with Paul at this time and
lost track of him for awhile, when he went to Paris in 1925 or
1926.

When he returned to America he drifted to New York and
lived in a tiny garret room in Greenwich Village, just off 6th
Avenue and 12th Street. The room, one of many cubicles
converted from an attic, was so close to the elevated trains
operating on 6th Avenue at that time that you could almost
touch the cars by stretching your arm out the window. The
racket was deafening. Paul paid three dollars a week for this

torture chamber and spent the remainder of his ten-dollar weekly stipend from his mother on food, tobacco and books. In a short time Paul and I resumed our friendship and began discussing the possibility of opening a bookshop in Milwaukee. The city had several bookshops that sold new books, but these shops were staid and conservative. We planned something entirely new: a rental library, the first in the city, and modern first editions. The more we considered it, the more interesting it became. We excitedly exchanged ideas and talked all day and long into the nights and finally arrived at the name of Casanova Booksellers and Importers.

Have you ever heard of a bookshop born in a beauty parlor? There have been bookshops born in restaurants, tearooms, saloons, antique shops and perhaps in other places but never, I believe, in a beauty parlor. In the month of October 1927, we opened the Casanova Bookshop in a tiny corner of The Downer Beauty Parlor, 591 Downer Avenue, adjacent to the barber, who eyed us with suspicion. If the barber was suspicious, one can surmise what the customers of the beauty parlor thought. Fortunately the ladies didn't know what Casanova meant or who he was. Paul and I had pondered a name for the bookshop over continuous chess games and finally settled upon Casanova. We both were fascinated with Casanova, whose *Memoirs* I had just read. We had contemplated other names like Argus, Argosy and other mythological names, and Chaucer, Shakespeare and names from classical literature. But the name Casanova sounded and seemed just right.

I continued in business under this name for ten years. But in 1937 I changed the name and wrote in the preface to my 10th Anniversary Catalog as follows: "With this catalog I have changed the name of my bookshop from Casanova to my own name. For ten years I have battled against American puritanism, innocently believing that the name of a bookshop was unimportant. I chose the name Casanova because I was sincerely interested in the man and his work, believing, as I still do, that he wrote one of the most fascinating autobiographies in world literature. However, the past ten years have convinced me that I have been operating against an insurmountable obstacle, prejudice. It is apparently still the American tradition to look upon the name Casanova with a grin. No serious person is supposed to read him, save secretly. And what Havelock Ellis wrote forty years ago, namely that 'Every properly constituted man of letters has always recognized that any public allusion to Casanova should begin and end with lofty moral reprobation of his unspeakable turpitude,' still remains today."

The insurmountable obstacle in getting a stock of books was our total lack of credit. We had no money, no collateral or property. We did not even have a bank account. It was under these circumstances that we wrote to one of the large book jobbers, A. C. McClurg & Co. in Chicago, ordering several hundred books and asking for 30 days' credit. We explained in our letter to the jobber that we were two young men who wanted zealously to become booksellers; that we had no money but were able and willing to work and were confident of success. We added in what appears now to be a facetious remark, that if they extended credit to us, we would in the future buy all our books from them. (We actually did this, and remained customers of A. C. McClurg & Co. until they went out of business.) The list of books we ordered was obtained from studying the *Publishers' Weekly* which we obtained at the Public Library, and ordering any new book which appeared to be suitable for our proposed rental library.

Not being too optimistic about acquiring the books from McClurg, we also ordered these same books from the individual publishers, making the same plea we had made to

McClurg. Our reasoning was that if we failed to obtain the books from McClurg we would at least get some books from the publishers. Our primary concern was to obtain books for the rental library. About a week following our order to Mc-Clurg, we received a telephone call from the credit manager of the big house, asking if we were playing some kind of joke on them; otherwise, what did we mean by ordering several hundred dollars worth of books on credit without exhibiting the faintest hint of our ability to pay for them, nor any credit references, bank account or anything else that is normally used in establishing credit. We repeated all that we had written but did add a significant statement of our intentions. We were planning to open the first rental library in Milwaukee; with free rent (from Paul's mother) and hardly any other overhead it would be difficult for us to fail. I repeated, almost pleaded, that we were young, intelligent and willing to work hard and very much wanted to become booksellers.

I think our rental library plans and my earnestness convinced the credit manager that we were worthy of a risk, because when I concluded talking to him, he intimated that they would send the books. Paul and I were elated and as luck would have it we also received some of our order from the publishers. Thus, from the very start, we had more books than we had counted on and there was only one course to pursue, which was to sell the books and pay for them promptly, which we proceeded to do. Although we knew little about operating a business, we surmised that credit was the most valuable part of any enterprise and although I had to borrow money from my mother to pay the express charges for the books from McClurg, I carefully arranged that the jobber was paid in full before the invoice was due.

We opened the shop with a modest rental library and our personal collection of first editions, which we pooled together.

The rental library was successful from the beginning and we persuaded some of the beauty parlor customers to buy a few books. To our astonishment and delight the beauty parlor turned out to be an excellent location for our bookshop. In the beginning, the only consideration was the free rent, because Paul's mother, as explained, leased the store. However, we discovered that many of the women who frequented the beauty parlor took a fancy to the rental library and became good customers. In less than a year we outgrew the corner in the beauty parlor and were ready to move into our own store. Fortunately a store was vacant just a few doors away and the rent was only $75 per month. We moved in.

But for one good idea, mentioned above, our shop might have foundered, as our friends so insistently had admonished us. And I still carried the memories of my trying experiences with Ward Moore and the Catacomb Bookshop in Chicago. However, our rental library rapidly developed into an extremely profitable venture. We charged a one-dollar membership fee and twenty-five cents per week per book. The membership fee gave us the required capital and we soon had over one thousand members. The membership fee was not returnable; it bought the privilege of renting books from our library. Although the idea of the rental library was not really a new idea at all, as there had been lending libraries in England for many years, it was new in America and particularly new in Milwaukee. (The first circulating or lending library was established in London in 1740.) We also made an important innovation, which was largely responsible for our initial success. Instead of supplying our customers with only the current best sellers, with the usual assortment of Western and Mystery, we decided to offer our members the best in Literature from all periods. We crowded our shelves with Proust, Gide, Mencken, Lawrence, Huxley, Powys, etc., and in addition we added all the current highbrow stuff. We would plunge with a book like *The Well of Loneliness*, of which at one time we had thirty copies in circulation. The book was banned by the Milwaukee Public Library and so we were virtually the only suppliers to the entire city. *The Well of Loneliness* became a sensational best seller. Tame by present-day standards, it was then regarded as containing the essence of pornography, although there was not a single four-letter word in it. It was suppressed in New York and the publishers merely moved its printing to New Jersey, from where it was shipped. It was hailed by reputable critics as the first significant homosexual novel, and that was really what all the fuss was about. A threatening incident occurred when we filled our entire display window with copies of this best-selling novel. It so happened that our store was not far from Downer College, a conservative private seminary for girls. The head of the English department of the school demanded that I remove the books from the window, stating that the book was obscene and the display provocative. I refused, claiming that the book was not obscene and citing the First Amendment and my own personal objection to censorship. She threatened me with a boycott of the students and faculty of the college. I told her to boycott if she wished but the books would remain in the display window, which they did. It required considerable gumption to take this strong position at this time. The faculty of the school were good customers; most of them were members of our rental library. But such is the courage or foolhardiness of youth that we refused any compromise with our strong beliefs.

The rental library continued to expand in the larger quarters and we began to invest the profits in antiquarian books and first editions. Our fame as a rental library had spread and we were now attracting readers from all parts of the city. Of

course, it had always been our intention to enter the antiquarian and first-edition business as quickly as we acquired
funds with which to buy books. Milwaukee in the late
nineteen-hundreds and during the first quarter of the new
century had been a good secondhand book town. At that time
there were several flourishing antiquarian bookshops in the
city.

In the beginning, our stock of first editions consisted of one
shelf with about fifty books. These were taken from our
personal libraries. People entering the bookshop would
curiously examine the prominent case labeled "First Editions"
and ask what the words meant. We tried to explain as inform-
ingly as we could. Those that indicated even the slightest
interest we were more painstaking with, and explained
patiently what first editions were and why. Some of these
expressed surprise that many of the books in the case were
marked up from their selling price. Again we explained the
reason for this. We lent to those who showed a little sympathy
for our hobby, books on book collecting, while others we
inspired with long, intimate talks on rare books. We devoured
catalogs and bibliographies, impatient to discover all that we
could about points and values.

Because the introduction to *This Book Collecting Racket*
so aptly records this period of our bookselling, I quote the
following: "In five years we have turned the tables. When we
opened our book shop in Milwaukee, there was not a single
collector of modern first editions in the city. The other booksellers contented themselves with selling school books and
best sellers. They saw little reason for trying to create a market
for first editions. The people want best sellers, they said; why
should we break our necks trying to sell them first editions?
They want Fannie Hurst, Kathleen Norris, Warwick Deeping,
and so on. It would be suicide to stock O'Flaherty, Faulkner,

Hemingway, Huxley, etc. Impertinence or suicide, or perhaps both. But we accomplished the seemingly impossible, and today we carry as large a stock of first editions as many metropolitan stores. Our local collectors can be counted in scores, and it is no trick for us today to sell fifty copies of a collected author in the first edition."*

My partnership with Paul did not proceed as smoothly as it appeared. We each brought an assortment of skills to the job. I was concerned with the practical side of operating the store. In buying books from a publisher, I liked to know to whom we might sell them; I also liked to assess whether we would sell many books or only a few. I endeavored to evaluate the potential of book sales in a realistic manner. Of course, I too got excited when I stumbled upon the then unknown William Faulkner's *Sanctuary* and ordered fifty copies, a big advance order for us at this time; or when I read the also unknown at the time *Tetralogy of Vardis Fisher* and bought all the limited, signed editions I could not afford. Also, one must remember that at this time a bookseller was unable to return any unsold books; what he bought he either sold, or if unsalable, was stuck with them. As a consequence, the buying of new, unknown authors could be quite hazardous.

Paul brought with him an impressive assortment of skills. He was enthusiastic, knowledgeable and an energetic worker. He was a good bookseller and as long as the economic conditions permitted, we performed well as a team. Last but not least, he was an able carpenter and built many of our ever-expanding book shelves. Paul, however, was also inclined to be a visionary. He would occasionally permit his enthusiasm to flee with his good sense. On these occasions,

---

* Quoted from *This Book Collecting Racket* by Harry W. Schwartz (Chicago, 1937).

when I discovered one of his lapses from reality, I would quietly ask our secretary Helen (who was Paul's wife) to mail a cancellation or scale down the size of an order.

The first year in our new location proved inordinately successful. We had opened our shop at the right psychological time. The location was excellent. We had no competition and even later, when rental libraries began to proliferate, our competition was negligible. Rental libraries have become so integrated with our culture that it is difficult to remember that less than fifty years ago there were none. And, of course, there were no paperbacks either. If you sought to read a new book, you either had to buy it or await your turn at the Public Library, which could be a long wait if the book were popular. There were reprints after one year or more of the best sellers and you could buy the numerous, inexpensive series like the Modern Library, Everyman's Library, World's Classics, etc., etc. Many publishers had their own reprint series, like Harcourt, Brace & Co. had its Harbrace, and Alfred A. Knopf had its Borzoi Editions, etc. At the present time the rental libraries are again disappearing, driven out by the paperbacks. But as the price of paperbacks advances and it becomes more expensive to buy a paperback than it does to rent a book, more people will patronize the rental libraries and we will witness a revival of this institution.

Our library business was booming and it appeared that we could never get enough first editions to satisfy the demand. Had Paul and I been smarter businessmen we might have averted the catastrophe which destroyed our business and ended our partnership. Or had we been spared a few more years, we might have weathered the depression, although it most probably would eventually have ruined us as it did so many others. Our antiquarian book business received a considerable boost when we bought the library of Mrs. Paul

Smith,* a good customer of the Downer Beauty Salon. I suppose every secondhand bookseller can pinpoint some episode in his career that gave him his initial start. I am not referring to the fact that someone died and money was inherited. I mean some fortunate transaction like being offered a large library at a low price; or obtaining some wealthy customers who like both you and rare books (like Dr. A. S. W. Rosenbach). In our case we were practically presented with the library of Mrs. Paul Smith. And indeed this was the library that established our business.

Mrs. Paul Smith was a wealthy widow who sold her large home on Lake Drive and moved into an apartment. It was one of the few homes, at that time, that could boast a separate room for a library which really contained shelving and books, and not just an expensive radio and clock and a little bookcase filled with knickknacks and just enough books to call it a library. True, the library consisted largely of Standard Sets, but sets that were the best available and that were exquisitely bound in morocco and calf. I remember sets of the limited Federal Editions and sets of limited editions of Thoreau, Burns, Plutarch, Scott, Dickens, etc. And, of course, as we were in our usual penniless situation, we could not offer what these books were worth. Also, one must remember that at this time Standard Sets were very difficult to sell. Rich people who formerly were the only customers for leather-bound sets had begun to sell their big houses and move into apartments. I knew that Mrs. Smith did not need the money, and I also knew how pitiably little money we had in the bank. Nor was there any way of borrowing money at this time. Consequently I offered her a low figure for the library. She accepted our offer, and we moved the books to our shop. We suspected that there

---

* A fictitious name.

was no local market for the sets, so we called several New York dealers who specialized in Standard Sets and sold them quickly at prices considerably lower than market value.

Our next important step in acquiring an antiquarian book stock was our purchase of the Dr. Horace Manchester Brown library. Dr. Brown was a peculiar, not a great, book collector. He bought anything interesting. Of course, Medicine was his main interest and his medical library was donated to the Marquette School of Medicine. We did not obtain any of his medical books. On his travels Brown visited old bookshops searching for interesting volumes. He became friendly with Pierre Louys, the celebrated French writer, and translated *The Songs of Bilitis* into English, which he had privately printed. In those days Louys was considered a writer of pornography and it was quite avant garde for a respectable American physician to do a translation of *Bilitis*. Louys' best-known works were *The Adventures of King Pausole* and *Aphrodite*, both of which were in our rental library.

Brown had ceased collecting books before we opened our shop and we never saw him before his death. I, of course, could not imagine that we would be so fortunate as to obtain the Brown library. I had heard of the library for years, and it was almost unbelievable when the widow called and asked me to look at the books. Brown lived in a big house on Prospect Avenue, one of the elite streets of the city at this time. I was ushered into a large room, the library, and left alone. I don't know why I always have a feeling of disappointment after I examine a library. Probably because I have imagined all kinds of rarities waiting for me and find none of them. The Brown library followed the same pattern; it turned out to be a strange conglomeration of esoteric books. Many of the titles were in a foreign language and I was unable to read them. I was dismayed. Was this really the great Brown collection that I had heard of for years? I searched further. I remember books on embalming in French; a sixteenth-century edition on wigs; books on demonology in various languages; books on arms and armor in Japanese; a tattered edition of Burton's *Arabian Nights*; etc., etc. Brown had the quaint habit of penciling in on the flyleaf the price, date of purchase and the name of the bookshop where he had bought the book. (This was great help in pricing the books.)

The sobering thought ran through my head that this stuff was unsalable in Milwaukee. Who would buy it? My customers were not scholars, and this was primarily a scholar's library. I would therefore have to rely upon a good news story and plenty of publicity to sell the books. I got more than enough of both. I explained to the widow that the books were curious and beyond the ordinary reader's interest, and therefore would be difficult to sell. I could only offer a low figure for their purchase. I walked around the room pointing to the odd titles and convinced her that very few people would want these books. She agreed with me. Moreover she wanted them removed as quickly as possible because they gave the room a musty odor. I obliged her.

With the books removed to our shop we got busy assorting and arranging some of the more interesting titles on tables. We then called the *Wisconsin News* and gave that newspaper the following story, which appeared on the evening of April 11, 1929: "The library of the late Dr. Horace Manchester Brown, one of the finest libraries in the country, not excepting those of Eastern book-collectors, is being cataloged at the Casanova Book Shop, 585 Downer Avenue, from which the books will be dispensed. Included in the library of several thousand volumes, which was purchased by the bookshop from the estate of Dr. Brown, are volumes on Art, Literature,

Music, Folklore and Travel. Many are the finest works of France, Italy, Spain and Germany, written in the native tongues of these countries and collected by Dr. Brown, apparently with little regard to the expenditures involved, during his travels. Also included in the library are many rare and valuable first editions and other items which are almost impossible to procure on the open market today. Most of these books contain notations in the margins, written by Dr. Brown, a man noted for his learning, and in many cases he has supplemented the thoughts of the author by contributions of his own."

This is where we made a disastrous blunder. We inadvertently used the words "rare" and "valuable" in describing the books to the reporters. We, of course, meant "rare" in the sense that they were strange and esoteric, not rare or valuable in any monetary sense. But alas, our preposterous exaggeration proved to have a treacherous result. The story printed in the *Wisconsin News* made it appear that we had obtained a rich, valuable and irreplaceable library. Of course none of this was true. Our publicity campaign had badly misfired. There was actually only one first edition of note in the entire collection. The Doctor had little interest in first editions. But when the newspaper story appeared, Mrs. Brown gathered from it that we had cheated her. I vainly attempted to explain that the newspaper story was a stupid exaggeration. She refused to listen to my explanations and in a rage scooped up an armful of books from the table, among which ironically was the only first edition in the entire collection, and dashed out of the store, threatening to have us arrested.

Alarmed at this turn of events we called our attorney and told him the story. Our attorney called the widow and explained that she must return the books. The widow's attorney also advised her to return the books. The attorneys had succeeded in convincing her that she was not cheated, that the newspaper story was a gross exaggeration, and that the books would really be difficult to sell. Mrs. Brown eventually returned the books by messenger. Our surmise that the books would be difficult to sell was borne out by experience. After more than ten years many of them remained unsold. I intended to discard some of the more tattered volumes but they gave the shop the appearance of being filled, even though few customers looked at them or could read the foreign titles if they did look. The Brown library had not been the pot of gold that we had hoped to find. But I was still hoping, as every antiquarian bookseller does, to uncover that elusive first edition of *Tamerlane* or *Bay Psalm Book* or even a *Leaves of Grass* concealed among the rubbish of an attic. I have traveled hundreds of miles in search of these rarities but regret to report I have never unearthed one.

One day, about twenty years ago, I received a long-distance telephone call from Cleveland, Ohio. A newspaper man was calling to tell me that his uncle had recently died in Beaver Dam, a small town in Wisconsin. He had been a recluse, so I was told, living in a big house filled with books. I received little information from the nephew except that I was to locate a real estate dealer in this small town who had the keys to the house and would allow me to examine the books. I thought that this seemed like a fitting background for a mystery story; however, there was no murder. The recluse had died at the age of 97 in the same house in which he was born.

The following Sunday I drove off on the hunt with my wife, who always accompanied me on my expeditions, our young son, and a bookselling friend, Jack Clapp, who was spending the weekend with us. It was a beautiful ride through the rich

Wisconsin farmlands, before the era of freeways and cement, when you could still observe the trees and cattle grazing in the fields. When we arrived in Beaver Dam and located our real estate agent, we drove to the house of the deceased recluse. Over the years I have grown accustomed to visiting homes in various stages of decay and ruin, but never have I seen anything resembling this wreck. Inside it was dark, although it was early afternoon on a bright, sunny day. And it was filthy. We immediately began searching through the mountain of books, coughing through the dust and grime. The books were stacked on shelves, on the floor, on stairs, window-sills, in closets and in drawers. But after the three of us searched for more than an hour, I realized that we were on another wild-goose chase. This fellow had bought to read, over the years, huge lots of cheap reprints. All the predecessors of Grosset and Dunlap, A. L. Burt, Donoghue, etc., were well represented in their flimsy cardboard bindings and yellowing, brittle pages. At the time I wondered why there were no original editions present. It occurred to me that the nephew had acquired all the good books before he called me, but the agent advised us that no one had removed anything from the house. It seemed incredible that of that huge pile of books so few should be desirable. But so it was, and so terminated another of our extravagant hopes of finding an old house full of first editions.

The following story appeared in the Milwaukee *Journal* recently, written by its Literary Editor, Leslie Cross:

> The shock that comes to a bookseller once in a lifetime came to Harry Schwartz one day last week. Answering the phone in his Wisconsin Avenue shop, he heard a voice announce calmly, "I have a first edition of the *Bay Psalm Book*. Are you interested?" Recovering from a sudden wave of faintness,

Harry assured his caller that indeed he was very interested.
He made an appointment to go to an East Side address the next
morning.

The *Bay Psalm Book*, in case you don't know, is the first book
(1640) printed in English in North America, and a copy brought
$151,000.00 recently at a New York auction. After a night of
wild surmise, Harry went to the address where lived a refined
old couple, obviously well-to-do. After some examination of
credentials, they brought into the living room a morocco-
bound ancient-looking volume. Leafing through it Harry
could find nothing wrong until he saw a watermark in the
paper. The book was a facsimile made in about 1890, value
possibly $10.00. "It happened to me only once in all these
years," Harry said, "I wouldn't survive a second time."

All my hunting for books did not end in failure. One
morning the telephone rang and the party calling was unable to communicate a message that was intelligible. It was
a voice with a strong foreign accent, but I was unable to
comprehend what the voice was expressing. I was on the
verge of hanging up in frustration when I asked for the
address from which the party was calling, where it appeared
there were some books, although what kind and how many
there was no way of determining. I was given an address
that was not far from our shop, so I jumped into my car
and drove to the address.

I found it was a large old apartment building. I searched for
the janitor and fortunately found him emerging from the
basement. I told him who I was and asked to look at the books.
He pointed toward the basement and motioned me into a room
which at one time had been used as a coal cellar. There I found
a barrel filled with books. It did not appear too auspicious as
I groped in the barrel and pulled out some books. I was
astounded. The first three books extracted were the Charles
Carrington edition of *Petronius* and a Hebrew dictionary in

two volumes. I turned to the janitor and asked whose books these were. With some difficulty I learned from his reply that they had belonged to one of the tenants who had died and the books remained in storage in the basement for many years. He was cleaning up because the building had been sold and he was eager to dispose of this junk. As he was talking and gesticulating I continued pulling books from the barrel. There were two more volumes of Carrington and more foreign dictionaries, rather a strange assortment.

Finally I reached the bottom of the barrel and asked how much he wanted for the books. He asked five dollars for his trouble and said he was going to give everything to the junkman anyway. Although I almost missed buying this collection, it was probably the most interesting small assemblage of books I had ever bought. I wondered what kind of book collector would buy both Charles Carrington editions and foreign dictionaries because Charles Carrington, at this time, was considered to be nothing but a publisher of pornography, which did not deter me from placing his books in my personal library, where they still are.

Charles Carrington started life as an errand boy and lavatory attendant. At age sixteen he was keeping a book barrow in Farrington Market, London. Carrington dominated the English Erotica book market from about 1895 to 1917. His most ambitious catalog (today a scarce collector's item) was called "Forbidden Books," an elegantly printed bibliography of books he had for sale. Among some of his most famous publications, all handsomely printed in limited editions, were: "Untrodden Fields of Anthropology" by Dr. Jacobus X; "The Lives of Fair and Gallant Ladies"; "The Secret Cabinet of History" by Dr. Cabanes; "Curious Bypaths of History," etc. In the Paris of the early twenties he became a pathetic figure. Blind as the result of syphilis, his predatory mistress stole all his books, stripped him of everything he possessed and finally consigned him to a lunatic asylum, where he died at age sixty-five.

It is curious that the two most famous publishers of Erotica ended their lives miserably. Isadore Liseux, an erudite ex-priest and bachelor bibliophile, published the great landmarks of Erotic Literature of earlier centuries, particularly the French and Italian. His books were issued in attractive editions and today are prized for their beauty. Instead of Liseux dying a wealthy man, as is sometimes alleged, he actually was found dead of starvation and cold in his bleak bookshop on the rue Bonaparte in Paris, eleventh of January 1894, at the age of fifty-eight.

The libraries we did not buy might have been more inter-esting and profitable than those we did buy. I received a phone call from a lady in Waukesha asking me to inspect her late husband's books. We drove out to the house and were told that the books were in the barn. I entered the barn, which was unlighted and windowless, and did my best to read the titles with the help of a flashlight. I was quite surprised, for although I had expected a collection of outcasts in the barn, I discovered many solid books which considerably perked up my interest. I asked the woman what she was asking for the collection of books. Here, I might interject, lies one of the hazards of bidding on libraries. One never knows whether the owner of the library is looking for a free appraisal or really wants to sell the books. For this reason I usually suggested to the library owners that if I did not buy the books I would charge a modest appraisal fee for looking at them and bidding on them. The widow balked at this suggestion and asked why I alone, of the three booksellers who had already examined the books, made this charge. From this I gathered that three booksellers had already bid on the books and that she was using the booksellers to bid against each other to raise the price. I certainly did not approve of this; moreover, I refused to bid on the collection rather than be treated as a shill at an auction.

Victor Berger was a socialist Congressman from Milwaukee and was the power behind the Socialist Party of the United States. It is sometimes forgotten that Milwaukee at the turn of the century was a bastion of Socialism. Berger was the only member of Congress who voted against the United States entering World War I. For this he was expelled from Congress. He was charged with sedition and sentenced to twenty years in prison. The sentence was reversed by the Supreme Court in 1921. He was allowed to take his seat in Congress and continued in the House until his death in 1929.

Berger had a large library but unfortunately it was in German. When Mrs. Berger died I was asked to bid on the books. I made a close inspection and confirmed that the books were in German, were largely about Socialism and would be difficult to sell. My German is imperfect and many of the titles were unknown to me. Consequently, although I had an abundance of light in contrast to the windowless barn that I have just described, I was really in the dark as to what I was looking at. I made an offer of $350 for the library, explaining the limited appeal of the books and the great difficulty I would have trying to sell them. The Berger son-in-law explained that he was offering the library to several Chicago dealers also and the highest bid would take it. Chicago outbid me and I lost the library. This was a severe blow as I felt I should have bought it and blamed myself for not bidding more.

We bought few books at auction, relying principally on private libraries to obtain our stock. We had one near disaster because of bidding at an auction. This was early in our career and it was the first auction to which we sent bids by mail. The sale was either at Christie's or Sotheby's in London. We stupidly placed our bids in the pounds column instead of the shillings column and, of course, we bought every book that we bid on. When we received our invoice and found that we owed several hundred pounds, instead of shillings, we were stunned. We certainly could not pay for the books and wrote to the auction house explaining our error and pleading inexperience. They accepted our explanation, although they rebuked us as only the British can rebuke.

CHAPTER IV

In all the official reference of the thirteenth and fourteenth centuries to the bookdealers, the ground is taken that they formed a class apart from mechanics or from traders in ordinary merchandise. They were considered to be engaged in an intellectual pursuit, and were treated as members of a profession....

GEORGE HAVEN PUTNAM

B ooks are sometimes like cats, which have a habit of suddenly turning up although you were certain you had got rid of them. Some years ago, I received a phone call from the late Joseph Padway, a well-known labor lawyer and national counsel for the A. F. of L. at the time. Judge Padway was a book collector whose library was sold at the Parke-Bernet Galleries following his death. Padway told me when he telephoned that he required a great many books in a hurry, but quickly added that they must be cheap. He didn't care what kind of books they were; they didn't even have to be in English. He wanted enough books to fill a wall measuring 30 feet long and 10 feet high. In other words he needed 300 square feet of books. It so happened that Padway had recently sold his home, which contained his excellent library. The people who bought the house knew nothing about books, but were impressed by his library and asked if the books went with the house. Padway answered that the books were his personal library, and that he had spent years collecting them. When the prospective buyers demurred, saying that they would not be able to fill the empty shelves, the Judge, eager to sell his home, offered to fill the shelves with books. He carefully explained that they would not be the same books as appeared there now, but they would be genuine books.

I had recently bought the Neil Norris library consisting of about 3,000 books, many of them worthless. Norris was a millionaire eccentric who lived with his mother in an enormous home on Wisconsin Avenue. The house was filled with books and after many local institutions, such as the Public Library, Marquette University, etc., were allowed to help themselves to what they could use, the balance was sold to me. My bookshop basement was overflowing and I urgently needed to get rid of some of the surplus books. Thus, when Padway made known his wants on the telephone, I exclaimed that I had just the books he needed. We bargained over the price of 300 square feet of books and finally agreed on ten cents per book.

A number of years elapsed and I had forgotten all about the Neil Norris books and about Padway and his books, too. In fact, the Judge had long since gone to the Happy Hunting Ground. One day I received a telephone call from a person who had a library for sale. I made an appointment to inspect the books. When I arrived at the prestigious address I was admitted and escorted to a spacious room filled with books. As I examined the titles I had an unnerving sensation of having seen these books somewhere. I continued looking and became convinced beyond a doubt that I had seen these identical books somewhere. At the same time something began to click in my memory. I called the lady of the house and asked her who had owned the house before she did. I was told that it had been owned by the late Judge Padway who, of course, had bought all these books from me and dutifully filled the shelves with them. I politely offered an excuse and departed from the house as quickly as possible.

Our first catalog, issued in the fall of 1931, although not a great financial success, earned us a minor reputation for bibliography. However, we were faced with a vexing problem: should we or should we not catalog a rare pamphlet, a quantity of which we had stumbled upon accidentally? Having already sold a copy to a collector in Philadelphia, we were worried that cataloging another copy so soon would make it appear that we had discovered a remainder of the rare pamphlet. This is the story of the pamphlet. One day my partner was poking about in a box of pamphlets at the C. N. Caspar Book Store when his eye lighted on a stack of Werner's Readings and Recitations No. 21, New York, 1899. Glancing through the pamphlet he found Kipling's *Sons of the Widow* and knew he had found a rarity. He quickly checked the box and found eight copies of the pamphlet in pristine condition. They were priced at 25 cents each and he bought all of them.

Back at our shop we hurriedly began our research and confirmed that we had found a rare Kipling item. Now the next step was to establish a price for this rarity. There was nothing to rely on. The item, to the best of our imperfect knowledge, had never been cataloged before nor had any copy ever been sold at auction. We had, a few years earlier, bought a copy of *Private Book Collectors of the U. S.* and looking through the book for Kipling collectors, we found one in Philadelphia. Now the problem was how much to charge for the pamphlet. We thought of a round sum of $100 or a small sum of $10. It seemed that anything presumed to be as rare as our pamphlet should not be sold for such a piddling sum as $10. We compromised and offered the pamphlet to our Kipling collector for $75. We were overjoyed to receive an immediate telegram ordering the pamphlet. This is a description of the pamphlet as item No. 133 in our first catalog issued in the Fall of 1931: "Kipling, Rudyard. Sons of the Widow. In Werner's Readings and Recitations, No. 21, 12mo. orig. cream wraps, N. Y., 1899, Fine condition, $75. To the best of our bibliographical knowledge we are offering the following information to those who are poorer or better informed than we are. There is only one other copy on record, sold by our firm to a Philadelphia collector. This is a very important Kipling item as it is the Only Publication in book form of this poem as it was originally written for its first appearance, which was in the *Scots Observer*, April 26, 1890. This is the poem called 'The Widow at Windsor,' which appeared in the first edition of *Barrack Room Ballads* under its altered title with several changes; as far as we know all reprintings have followed the altered form. According to the authorities, this poem (an attack on Queen Victoria) is the reason Kipling has never been appointed Poet Laureate when opportunities for such an appointment have presented themselves to the King."

Although the rental library was still profitable it had begun to suffer from the inroads of numerous small competing lending libraries that had opened around us. None of these could compare, whether in selection of books or service, to our library but every one nibbled a few of our customers away. When the depression hit us full force we were staggered. First we lost most of our customers for first editions and rare books. Then we found ourselves loaded with books that we could not sell. Worst of all these books had been bought at high prices. Many of our customers were unable to pay their bills, which made it difficult, if not impossible, for us to meet our own payments. We began to examine what other possibilities existed to bring in additional revenue and fell upon the idea of adding pornography to our rental library.

Pornography in those days was something clandestine and furtive, like bootlegging. Everybody, or almost everybody, drank bootleg whiskey but there was something more than illicit about pornography. It was believed to be degrading. The finest people drank illegal booze, and some of the best customers of speakeasys were among them; but only perverts and degenerates were supposed to read pornography. Imagine Sir Richard Burton returning to earth today and finding his *Kama Sutra* or his *Perfumed Garden* on sale at bargain prices, in some instances less than one dollar. (Lady Burton burned the manuscript of the latter expanded version of *The Perfumed Garden*; the edition now available is the one Burton published in 1886 without the annotations, which were presumed to be his magnum opus.) And what would Frank Harris say upon returning from the only place he could have gone to, to find his *Life and Loves* on sale in a paperback at $1.65? This is the book that three countries, including the United States, persecuted him for publishing and burned all the copies they could seize. But the most amazing of all is to find the notorious *Fanny Hill* on sale in a paperback at 95 cents. This is the lascivious eighteenth-century novel that sent more booksellers to jail than any book ever published. I will have more to say about this book in a later chapter.

We began our pornographic rental library, I believe the first one in existence at that time, with about one hundred books. These contained the standard titles of pornography with the addition of some scholarly books about sex and related subjects. Among the titles were the following: *My Secret Life, Memoirs of a Russian Princess, The Autobiography of a Flea, Venus in India, Romance of My Alcove*, etc. Once more we were able to escape the effects of the depression with considerable revenue from our pornographic library. Of course we were cautious and loaned books only to people we knew. It was revealing to discover that some of our leading citizens were among our best customers. One unexpected result of our

pornographic rental library was developing a millionaire customer who wished to buy the books instead of renting them.
Naturally we were willing to accommodate this millionaire
and for a considerable period of time this customer was the
financial pillar of our business.

Managing our bookshop, buying the new books and pur-
chasing private libraries kept us busy but we usually found
time to read. One of the main reasons for having gone into the
book business was because I liked to read. At an early period
I realized that you must read books to be able to sell them.
Books that you have read yourself can be recommended,
providing you found them interesting, with an enthusiasm and
sincerity that reading numbers of book reviews will not im-
part. I found that if you wanted to sell a book in quantity, you
must read it yourself. I do not mean reading a mystery or a
western or even a best seller. These books don't require any
selling as they are usually pre-sold. I am recalling how I sold
fifty copies of Faulkner's *Sanctuary* at a time when few people
had even heard of his name. I had been reading Faulkner for
some time and although, at this period, none of his books sold
well, I had personally found them interesting. *Soldiers Pay*
and *Mosquitoes*, both published by Horace Liveright, were
remaindered. I remember selling them at 39 cents each on my
bargain table. (My copies of the first edition sold at the
Parke-Bernet Galleries in 1963 brought one hundred and
seventy dollars respectively.) However, when *Sanctuary* was
published, and I read it immediately, I decided to write a letter
to all my customers who I had interested in first editions of
contemporary authors. I wish I had a copy of this letter today,
because I believe this was the first time that anyone hailed
Faulkner as a literary giant and predicted a great collecting
future for him. In fact, my partner and I were so smitten with
Faulkner that we decided we had to publish something by him.

It was presumptuous of us to ask him to give us something to publish, but one night we sat in a little Italian speakeasy drinking a concoction called Dago Red, which was homemade wine spiked liberally with alcohol, when the idea of publishing something by Faulkner became the topic of conversation. We decided to write him then and there, but we had no paper. We used the paper napkins on our table and with the help of the spiked wine composed a letter that was both flattering and entertaining. Faulkner apparently found the napkins amusing too, because he offered us the "Double Dealer" material, which we published under the name of *Salmagundi*. The Hemingway poem got into the book only because it happened to be on the same page of the Double Dealer as the Faulkner material. Today *Salmagundi* is a very rare book and worth about $300. It was published in 1931 in a limited edition of 300 copies at $3.00 per copy.

However, the depression continued and as quickly as our wealthy customers' income was threatened, which was inevitable, our business collapsed. It seemed as though all our customers stopped buying books at precisely the same time. The end of '31 and beginning of '32 was really the start of the depression for us. It was practically impossible to sell a book, and even if you sold one, it was impossible to get any money. Our accounts receivable began to bulge with unpaid bills. And, of course, some of our customers took advantage of poor little schnooks like us. One customer, as an example, a rich socialite, owed me nearly one thousand dollars, but I was unable to get any money out of her. This woman had been a good customer for several years. Her bills were always late in payment but eventually she did pay them. However, this time she ignored all requests for payment. The statements and letters sent to her were unanswered. Whenever I called her on the telephone I was rebuffed. Finally my patience was exhausted and the need for money was desperate, so I called my attorney for advice. He suggested a law suit, but I was opposed to this. The woman was, after all, a millionaire, and how does one go about suing a millionaire for a comparatively small sum of money? My attorney then proposed that I write her husband, who was a prominent businessman, and tell him that his wife owed me money which I was unable to collect, and that I wanted his help to get it. I sat down immediately and wrote a straight-forward letter to her husband. I had a check for the amount of the account within twenty-four hours, but I lost Mrs. _____ as a customer.

Now set in a period of depression such as I had never before experienced. To cut expenses still further I moved out of a small apartment I had formerly rented and occupied a tiny room at the back of the bookstore. This room had barely enough room for a bed, but it was warm and cost me nothing. Oddly enough, it had a skylight which brought in the sun at the crack of dawn, a pleasure which I did not always appreciate.

Directly in the rear of this "bedroom" was a shed which I used for storage. Unfortunately, it also housed rats, and at night you could hear them scurry around outside my door. This shed was to cause me considerable trouble. The roof leaked and the rats ate the glue off the books. But a bigger nuisance was to follow. One day a tall, seedy man entered the store and told me he was a bookseller scout. He added that he was hard up (who wasn't) and asked if he could sleep in the shed which he observed in the rear of the bookstore. He had already parked his old jalopy in my parking lot at the back of the shed. It would only be for a night or two, while he scouted the Catholic Schools and monasteries for Catholic Encyclopedias which he specialized in. Against my better judgment I allowed him to move in, providing he refrained from smoking in the shed.

How could I refuse a poor bookseller a roof over his head, even though he had to share it with rats? However, when the one or two nights stretched into three months, I locked the shed and that was the last I saw of the book scout.

Was there some meaning to bookselling that I could not fathom? I was a good salesman and even in the depression years it was possible to obtain some work, so why did I pursue this near bankrupt business? These are questions that many booksellers must have asked themselves in the past. There probably is no simple answer to this age-old question. Each person must find something in her or his work which compensates for all the poverty, frustrations and loneliness with which he is confronted. Certainly the desire for gain alone could not be the purpose, because very little profit was expected.

For that matter, why should a novelist labor for two years and more on a book only to find it remaindered after selling a few hundred copies? Ford Maddox Ford in a letter to H. G. Wells observed that after three months of publication his book had only received five reviews, three of them in provincial papers, and that as far as he could determine, only four copies of the book had been sold. Of course this lack of sales discouraged Ford, but he did not quit. To the contrary, he wrote and published more than ever. In a span of six years, from 1905–1910, he published 18 books, and during his lifetime he published no fewer than 80 books. I believe that Christopher Morley, who published 70 books in twelve years, held the record, but I find that, so far as I know, it belongs to Ford.

Perhaps I should digress for a minute and say something about bookselling in the 1920s and 1930s. In *This Book Collecting Racket* I criticized the method by which first editions were sold. If a bookseller wanted five copies of a first edition of a particular author it was necessary to order twenty-five copies. Of many limited editions it was impossible to obtain a single copy. Frequently we ordered ten and some-times fifty copies of a Golden Cockerel or Nonesuch Press title, and believed ourselves fortunate if we obtained two or three copies. It was positively senseless. Time and again I was warned by our London agent, William Jackson, Ltd., that if I wanted a few copies of a limited edition I should never order less than a dozen. All orders for first editions of collected authors like Cabell, Galsworthy, D. H. Lawrence and Joyce were rationed. Some limited editions sold at a premium even before they were published. Many well-known authors were issued in unbelievably expensive editions. Joseph Conrad's slight story *The Sisters*, a few pages long, was published by Crosby Gaige at $20 a copy and the entire edition was over-subscribed. Because Mr. Percy Muir has summed this up so well in his article "Some Book Collecting Blind Alleys" in an issue of *The American Book Collector*, I quote a few paragraphs:

> First novels are now published with a flourish of trumpets and a chorus of praise for a genius combining the greatness of Fielding, Bronte and Thackeray in one person. These paeans seem a little shrill and hysterical when applied to pseudo-Freudian interpretations of the rather nauseating family circle of Mr. Somebody-or-others extreme youth. The truth is, of course, that the publishers have decided to muscle in on the first-edition racket. The time is overdue when the collector should show the publisher clearly and unmistakably where he gets off. The first-edition business is no concern whatsoever of the publisher, and his clumsy method of barging into it should be made to produce effects beyond the depletion of the collector's pocket, to which it is at present limited. Any extension of the extraordinary practice of producing first editions ready made, high prices, rarity artificially produced (some books are as rare as First Folios as soon as they are published) and everything all complete, should be sat on, and the book collector is the only person who can do it.

I refer, of course, to the misbegotten monstrosity which calls itself a limited edition, and goes on calling itself such even when there are three thousand of it. Is this not racketeering with a vengeance? I have instanced in another place, the bludgeoning tactics which produce a limited edition before the trade edition. But authors are awkward fellows who do not always work to time. They promise to sign the sheets by a certain date and then go off and find something better to do with their pens than signing their names a thousand times or more. On the other hand the collector is a trusting and accommodating person. If a publisher tells him that a limited edition appeared before the trade edition, it will never enter his head that the publisher will deceive him. It seems incredible that publishers should sink to such a thing, but in the past few years there are at least two cases of a reputable publisher printing a bibliographical note which states that the limited edition appeared before the ordinary, when in fact, precisely the opposite occurred . . . . There is another perfectly sound reason for limited editions and it is professedly at the back of most of them that are produced. It is argued that (a) the first trade edition of a popular book is so large that the first edition of it tends to lose importance in the eyes of the collector and (b) that if the collector is prepared to pay a high price in order to have his books printed on good paper and well bound there can be no objection to catering to him.

The first of these two arguments seems to me to be specious. It falls before the objection of artificially manufacturing a first edition market, and it is seldom, in point of fact, that this sort of limited edition holds its own price. The salesrooms are littered with them, and they can be bought for half their published price or less. The second argument would be sound if its provisions were unexceptionably observed.

Mr. Moore's imitation parchment and Mr. Galsworthy's limp lambskins are not noteworthy examples of fine book production or likely to last longer than the cloth covers of the trade edition. And if Mr. Orioli expects us to pay twenty-five shillings for three-and-six-penny worth of text and six-penny worth of illustrations of Lawrence's early life, he should make it up to us in paper and binding. But, does he? Not a bit of it. We dare not open the book for fear of breaking its back or soiling its cover. A limited edition of a collected author was recently published in America at about ten dollars, the contents of which consisted of twenty-four pages. Of these twenty-four, three contained text, fifteen were blank, and the rest were given to title page, certificates of limitation and the like.

The great depression as it affected our book business was misleading and consequently, in the beginning, we were hardly aware of it. Following the crash of the stock market in the fall of 1929, our business, paradoxically, was more prosperous than ever. And during the years of 1930 and 1931 our sales reached a five-year peak. Because of this prosperity in the midst of a depression we made no attempt to cut back our buying or reduce our obligations. Had we displayed a little caution we would have put some cash into a reserve fund against the oncoming bad times. But we were fooled by the excellent sales and gave little heed for the future. We couldn't understand why people were complaining when our business was better than ever. Of course, this seeming paradox was easily explained had we not been so inexperienced and naive. It was simply that our customers were amongst the wealthy whose income had not yet been disturbed, and who could still afford to buy rare books and first editions.

Leafing through a catalog of British remainders one day, I happened upon an item that interested me. It was this: A. S. W. Rosenbach, *The Unpublishable Memoirs*, London, John Castle, N. D. 1/6. This was a collection of seven stories about a delightful book collector named Robert Hooker. I had read the book some years previously when I devoured everything that the Doctor had written about book collecting. And it was only recently that I had read that a copy of Rosenbach's *The Unpublishable Memoirs* had brought sixteen dollars at an American auction. I knew that the book had been published by Mitchell Kennerley in America in 1924 and was now out-of-print. I did not know that it had been published in England and remaindered.

I immediately sent a cable to England inquiring how many copies were available and a price for the entire lot. A cable reply advised me that there were 400 copies and I could have the entire lot for one shilling each. I bought them all and advertised them in the New York Times Book Supplement at $1.00 each. My little nuggets sold so fast that I increased the price to $2.00 each. I have only one copy remaining now and that one is in my personal library. Even the remainder is now a scarce book.

Another item on which I made a substantial profit was a book that is a rarity today and almost unobtainable. It is *Sherwood Anderson and Other Famous Creoles.* (This is a book of drawings by William Spratling, with a foreword by W. F. (William Faulkner). Caricatures of Anderson, Roark Bradford, Faulkner and 38 others. New Orleans, 1926. Limited to 150 copies.) I have forgotten how or from whom we acquired these, but my scrapbook notes that it was in 1931. The price must have been low because we priced them to sell at $2.25 per copy. This little book developed quite a bibliographical problem and we devoted an entire page of our first catalog of Modern First Editions, Fall 1931, to the various issues of this rare Faulkner item. In the catalog we advanced the price to $4.00.

Another remainder which brought us a nice profit was the first book written by John Dos Passos. It was called *One Man's Initiation* and was first published in England in 1920. The American edition did not appear until 1922, one year after the *Three Soldiers*, which was published in 1921. We cataloged it at $1.50. Today it is a scarce book and brings many times that amount. In a letter from Dos Passos he writes me as follows: "For some reason my memory is blank about how *One Man's Initiation* got to Allen and Unwin. I don't think it ever got shown to an American publisher, or if it did, it was part of another novel that has never come out. And never will. That and *The Garbage Man* were parts of an unfulfilled childish project I was working on in Spain at the time, and it seemed easier to try it in England where there was much more freedom of expression about the war than in Mr. Wilson's America."

Our shop was tiny compared to the bookshops I had known in New York, but what we lacked in size and stock we made up for in energy. On most any day I and my partner Paul would be busy cataloging books recently purchased; working on bibliographies (our firm issued three series of *Check Lists of Modern Authors*); working on our catalogs, which were models of their kind, and are now collected; writing long letters to customers and talking. People came to the shop first out of curiosity, and many returned. There was always a chess board handy and some of our customers stopped to talk and play.

Still another aspect of bookselling in the 1930s was the book thief who was ushered in by the huge demand for "high spots." They were called "high spots" because they were supposedly the important first editions that every collector should have in his library. Many collectors took this dictum at precise face value and would buy nothing but "high spots." In fact, it became so fashionable to collect high spots that a rare bookseller could sell nothing else, although his shelves were bulging with good first editions. And, of course, this sent the prices for high spots soaring. To fill this demand for high spots book thieves got busy. Book-crook rings in New York and elsewhere sent out thieves to despoil public and private libraries. These human bookworms were given a list of high spots and were told to filch copies of the first editions; a brief description was written out for them so they would have little difficulty in identifying them. These thieves scoured the small public libraries on the Atlantic coast and invaded the large private libraries of the universities.

The stolen rare books were brought to the "fence," where they were in turn sent to an expert bookbinder. The binder removed all telltale labels and through a clever process, smoothed out the perforations. Where a book consisted of several issues, copies were frequently "faked." This was accomplished by removing or inserting advertising; taking a poor copy of a first edition, first issue apart and substituting its pages with the "points" for the wrong pages in a fine copy of the second issue; totally recasing a book where the points are part of the binding; and a score of other tricks. These books were then supplied to accomplices in the book trade who eased them off on dealers and unsuspecting collectors.

Let me say here that the collector was frequently deserving of being duped. For instead of patronizing honest dealers who guaranteed their books, he was led to purchase, at a lower price, books from fly-by-night dealers, or unreliable individuals. To make a saving of several dollars, he made an investment that was worthless, and ironically, he really encouraged the thieves in their operations. For it is reasonable to assume that if the thief could not successfully sell his spurious rarities he would not traffic in them. I narrowly escaped from being unwittingly involved with a ring of book thieves myself. The leader of this ring of thieves was a bookseller named Charles Romm. He was sentenced to the penitentiary for a term of three years, charged with being at the head of a group of library thieves who stole, over a period of three years, rare books valued at $40,000. I knew Romm when he was perhaps a poorer but an honest man, in the days when he operated a basement bookshop somewhere along Fourth Avenue in New York. We often played chess together. Some years later, on a buying trip to New York, I was surprised upon walking into a bookshop to find Romm greeting me. I had almost forgotten him. I told him what my business was in New York, and he asked me to follow him into a back room. Lo and behold! I found myself in a veritable treasure-house of rarities. I looked for Romm to ask him where he got the money to assemble this fine lot. He had left me alone, so I began to examine the books carefully. Frequently I found three and four copies of the books in the first edition then being sought by most dealers. There were the early Cabells, Byrne, Dreiser, Morley, Robinson, etc. I selected a group of about thirty books and told Romm to hold them for me until the following day, as I did not have enough cash with me. As I left Romm's shop the thought struck me: Why do other dealers not know about this cache? Moreover, I thought the prices were extremely reasonable and wondered why other dealers had not snapped them up.

The following day I had lunch with another bookselling friend and casually mentioned Romm and the fact that I had selected some good buys at his shop. My friend excitedly reached across the table and grabbed my arm, demanding I tell him if I had bought anything there. I answered in astonishment that I had not. My friend said, "Every book you saw in Romm's shop was stolen. If you were not a trusting fool you would know they were stolen. Do you think that all the booksellers in New York are stupid? He has thousands of dollars worth of rare books in that room and every one of them was stolen from a library." I asked him, if this was true, why did the dealers not report him? He said that the dealers all knew about it but did not want to get messed up in the affair, but he would get caught sooner or later.

CHAPTER V

Are we not driven to the conclusion that of all things which man can do or make here below, by far the most momentous, wonderful, and worthy are the things called Books?

THOMAS CARLYLE

However, with all our ingenuity, we could not make a go of it. As the depression deepened we sank steadily into debt and our partnership was soon to be dissolved. My partner had a wife and two children and I thought it only fair and equitable that he should acquire the store. He required a continuous income and although it had dwindled considerably, the rental library and what other business remained could support one family. We decided that $500 and some books was all the business was worth. My partner promised to obtain this sum, and with the $500 in view, I began making plans to go to Tahiti with Don Smith and his wife Tamma, friends I had made in the bookstore.

But alas, Paul was unable to raise the money and not wishing to be a burden on my friends, who generously offered to pay my fare to Tahiti, I remained in Milwaukee. My mother loaned me $500 and I became the sole proprietor of Casanova Booksellers. We were in the third year of the great depression, and if I thought that we had already passed through the most difficult period, I was quickly disillusioned. We had not come close to touching bottom and from now on conditions really became rough. Nobody honored any bills and together with the publishers' demands to pay up, they also now threatened to throw me into bankruptcy.

My first-edition business had by this time substantially
declined and my only source of income was the rental library.
I struggled on because I have a stubborn streak that does not
quit easily. However, I realized that the first-edition business was exhausted in Milwaukee. Many of my customers lost
their enthusiasm for first editions when the depression hit
them. Others, having taken large losses in the stock market,
felt that they could not afford the luxury of collecting books.
Also, there was a serious problem of supply. One had to be
near the auction market for rare books, which was New York.
Chicago had a limited auction market and I attended the sales
there, but I knew that this could only be a half measure. You
had to be where the market was to engage successfully in the
rare-book business. Moreover, I had very little money and a
rare-book business needs capital. Most of my tiny capital was
frozen in my stock. At this juncture I decided to move my store
downtown and enter the new-book business. The decision was
a difficult one to make because it required that I sell the only
profitable part of my business, which was the rental library.

Now there developed another complication which added to
my difficulties and made the sale of the rental library impera-
tive. I had some months earlier, about September 1, 1937,
signed a three-year lease for the premises on Downer Avenue.
But the lease carried a clause, quite common at that time, that
the landlord was able to cancel the lease upon thirty days'
written notice. It was not much of a lease, but the best I could
negotiate at the time. All my Christmas cards had been bought
and delivered and all my fall books were in the store when my
landlord (the National Tea Co.) served me with a writ to vacate
the store in thirty days. Hardly anything worse could have
happened because there were no store vacancies in the neighborhood at this particular time and the store was jammed with
Christmas cards and merchandise. Moreover, and by far the

most important, what was to become of the rental library, which was the most valuable part of my business? All my pleadings for an extension of time were ignored. The landlord refused to explain why he wanted me out, but later I learned that he had rented the store to a chain hosiery shop at a sharp increase in rent. A neighborhood rental library cannot be moved out of the neighborhood without losing a substantial number of customers. Some customers will follow you wherever you go but the majority will not. Of course, you will acquire some readers in a new residential neighborhood, but our location on Downer Avenue had become so well established over the years that it would be difficult to find another location to equal it. The only location that was available and that I felt gave promise of developing into a good rental library was Capitol Drive and Oakland Avenue. I rented a store, moved in and immediately put the rental library up for sale. The need for capital was now acute and the thousand dollars that I asked for the rental library, although a small sum, was a godsend. I sold it within a week to an ex-schoolteacher and although I regretted selling it, I was also relieved.

Somehow the idea has circulated that all landlords are skinflints, mean and unfeeling rascals. And the richer the landlord the meaner and more unscrupulous he is. This, as other generalizations, has not proven true in my own case; in fact, just the opposite has been my experience.

The only landlord that had given me any trouble was the National Tea Co., which owned the first building that we occupied on Downer Avenue. When our lease expired they forced me to move with a month's notice, without giving me the opportunity to meet the increased rent they were asking for the store. They lied to me, telling me that the building was to be demolished. This was not true; they only wanted more rent. When we moved to Sixth and Wisconsin Avenue, we rented from a member of the Uihlein family. In spite of all the vicious accusations that have been made against the Uihleins, I found them considerate landlords. While other building owners were charging all that the traffic would bear, Uihlein, aware that he was renting an old building with many deficiencies, charged only a modest rental. He could easily have charged twice as much rent and every tenant would have gladly paid it.

When the building was finally demolished we had been tenants for ten years. During this period our rent had not been increased once. When the building was finally torn down, to make room for the Downtowner Hotel, we again had a multimillionaire for a landlord. Here again we were treated with consideration and the landlord went out of his way to be helpful. Of course, we had been good tenants, realizing that if we wanted favors from the landlord we should be deserving of them. We always paid our rent promptly and scrupulously performed all our obligations in our lease.

Our move downtown was not exactly auspicious. Our first location was poor, although the rent was cheap. I still was to learn that in this world you get exactly what you pay for: a low rental equals a poor location. In a desperate attempt to raise more capital I offered to sell my rare books to a large Chicago dealer. However, his price was so low that I decided to retain my books and struggle along without the capital I so urgently needed. Many of my books were obtained from the British jobber previously mentioned, named William Jackson Ltd. This firm had been lenient with me and during various times I owed them considerable sums of money. Suddenly, at the moment when I owed them a substantial sum and when the British pound, which had been fluctuating between three and four dollars, jumped to nearly seven dollars they decided to put the screws to me and threatened me with bankruptcy at approximately the same time a number of American publishers began threatening.

Many businessmen were taking advantage of the bankruptcy laws by closing their shops or offices and declaring bankruptcy. Following this, the merchandise or whatever was sold at auction by the court to the highest bidder. It was then an easy matter for the bankrupt to buy back the stock and assets for a fraction of their value. This was because nobody wanted these assets anyway, and very few people had any money to bid on them even if they did want them. The only problem was that the bankrupt was not supposed to have any money either. To bypass this legal block it was usually arranged that the bankrupt have a friend or relative bid for him. Then, when the business was recovered through these shenanigans, it was returned to the bankrupt, who now was in possession of a debt-free business. Of course, it was expected that the bankrupt would pay a small "fee" to the friend or relative.

It was suggested that I take advantage of this scheme to extricate myself from my debts, but I refused. It seemed to me, at this time, that this was a dishonest practice. I felt a moral obligation to pay my debts in full, if only the harassing creditors would give me time to do so. But this the publishers persistently refused to do. Each time that I pleaded for an extension, they would threaten me anew. One of the most demanding publishers was Alfred A. Knopf, who had built a reputation for publishing books of the sort that frequently became collectors' items. Thus it happened that I owed this publisher a larger sum of money than most of the others. This publisher tried his utmost to force me into bankruptcy, proving that it is possible to have a heart of stone and an excellent taste for literature at the same time. I wrote a long letter to the attorney representing the publishers, explaining my position in detail and offering to pay all my obligations, provided I was given the opportunity to do so. The only alternative was bankruptcy and the publishers could expect little or nothing in return.

Looking back at this period forty years later, it seems strange that one single incident, the great depression, had conditioned one's entire life. In fact, I was never the same again. Opportunities slipped by because I was too preoccupied with security. Offers were ignored because of fear of another depression. New ventures became possible, but in each case I was frightened off by specters of the past. This became a subconscious fear that took possession of you and molded all your actions. At moments you might free yourself from this albatross, do something daring, only to have the fears return and stifle any action you had planned.

The store we had moved into was on the fringe of the downtown area at 723 W. Wisconsin Avenue and almost directly across the street from the public library. But, alas, people who borrow books from the public library are not book buyers, as we discovered quickly. However, the store did have a huge rear room which we converted into an art gallery, where we held regular exhibits of Wisconsin artists. We were the first and only commercial art gallery of this kind in the city. The gallery did little business but it was fun to plan the shows and talk with the people who came to view the paintings. Together with the bookstore it was a failure. Fortunately we had only a three-year lease.

There was, however, one successful show (although we made no money on it) which consisted of an auction for Republican Spain. For this event I gathered all the donations I could get. It was heartwarming the way most artists, although poor themselves, sympathetically offered their work for this occasion. We obtained maximum publicity for the show and served refreshments, and for the first time the gallery was jammed with people. But although the crowd was enthusiastic, it lacked money. Everybody took a hand at auctioneering and we did succeed in raising several hundred dollars for Spain.

Very shortly, the war clouds in Europe began to darken and it seemed it would be just a brief time before we too would be embroiled in it. At about this time, 1940, we had a piece of good luck; a store in a better location became available at the same rent we were paying and we moved in. This was at 607 W. Wisconsin Avenue.

Shortly after we moved into our new location, which I hoped would be an improvement over the old one, I received a telephone call from New York from Horace Gardner. Horace was the sales manager for A. S. Barnes & Co., principally a publisher of sports books. He was one of my favorite salesmen. He was pudgy, no longer young and had a wonderful sense of humor. He was almost totally deaf, and you had to shout to make yourself heard. Horace wore a hearing aid but invariably had the gadget turned off or else the battery was dead. He hated it. The conversation with Horace went something like this: "Hello, Harry, this is Horace Gardner, how are you fella? I want you to have an autographing party for one of our authors. I am sending you 500 copies of *My Life with the Redskins* by Corinne Griffith, the well-known movie star. The Redskins, as you know, are playing the Green Bay Packers on Sunday and I want you to have the party on the Saturday before the game. I am shipping the books by express and John Marshall (husband of Corinne Griffith and manager of the Redskins) will bring the team into the store. It will be a round robin autographing, and you should have a big round table to seat the team, all of whom will autograph the book. Harry, call the *Journal* and the *Sentinel*

(our morning and evening newspapers) and place advertisements for the party. Call the sports editors of both papers and
alert them for stories, reviews, etc. Barnes will pay for everything. Harry, this should be big." And with this spiel he hung
up. I tried to stop him and yelled "Horace, Horace, wait a
minute." But it was useless. Horace did not give me an
opportunity to refuse.

My ears were still ringing, for as usual people who are hard
of hearing shout into the telephone. What to do now? My first
impulse was to call Horace and cancel the party before he
shipped the books. Who remembered Corinne Griffith, who
was a movie star twenty-five years ago? On the other hand, it
just possibly might succeed. Besides, we were spending none
of our own money and getting valuable publicity.

I decided to go ahead with the party. We had posters lettered
for the windows and big streamers screaming that the
Redskins were coming. We placed advertisements in both
papers, borrowed a big round table and chairs and even
borrowed a phonograph to play the team's theme song. (This
resulted in an unanticipated catastrophe because we burned
out the motor of the machine, which operated on A.C. current
while the store used D.C. current.) Finally the day of the party
arrived. I had one of our big windows filled with books for a
week and now we removed them to the round table where they
were piled in huge stacks.

At eleven o'clock on Saturday morning the Redskins,
Corinne Griffith, and Marshall came into the store. I shook
hands with all of them and escorted them to the round table
where they began autographing books. Miss Griffith had a
cold; her nose was running and she needed Kleenex. I fetched
her a box. Meanwhile big John Marshall walked up and down
the store smoking a long cigar. The store was unusually quiet
for a Saturday morning even without the autographing party.

Time passed. Nobody came near the autographing table, which was at the rear of the store. I began to get nervous. At a quarter to twelve I was beginning to suspect disaster. When at 12:15 still nobody bought a book I suggested to Mr. Marshall that enough copies were autographed and he and Miss Griffith and the team should leave. Marshall, unperturbed by the lack of sales, said "Mr. Schwartz, I promised Horace I would sign all these damn copies and by God I intend to do just that." I tried to hide but unfortunately our store had no hiding place. I began taking inventory, anything, to keep busy and distant from Marshall who smoked one cigar after another. About a quarter after one a little black lad came into the store and shyly asked if he could shake the hand of Sammy Baugh, the Redskins' big Texan quarterback. Finally, even Mr. Marshall agreed that enough copies had been signed and Miss Griffith was getting tired. They mercifully called it off and left. I was exhausted and believed that I was about to experience a nervous breakdown. This autographing party left such a traumatic scar that it was years before I could tolerate the thought of having another one.

The following article, "No, the McGuffey Readers are Not Dead," appeared in the *Publishers' Weekly* of January 1, 1962.* I reprint it here because it illustrates how an alert bookseller can turn a local event into an unexpected profit:

> This is a fantastic story about the old McGuffey Readers. For some booksellers to whom the McGuffey reader is merely the title of an old school book I should like to add a few words of explanation. Many years ago, when I was in the old and rare book business I would occasionally obtain McGuffey readers in the

---

* Reprinted from the January 1, 1962 issue of the *Publishers' Weekly*, published by the R. R. Bowker Co. (after January 1968) a Xerox Corp. Copyright 1962 by R. R. Bowker Co./Xerox Corp.

purchase of private libraries. These readers, which at that time were common because millions of them had been issued (more than 120 million copies had been sold in various editions in the United States), were usually sold at 50 cents to $2.00. However, as it became more difficult to purchase old libraries, old Mc-Guffey Readers became scarce, and the demand for them seemed to decline also. We would now and then get a request for them from a collector of old children's books and that was about all. The McGuffey Readers were practically dead as far as sales were concerned, and although we knew that reprints were available, we didn't bother with them. And then all of a sudden, practically overnight, the entire picture changed. This is what happened....

The Twin Lakes (Kenosha County, Wisconsin) school board adopted the McGuffey Readers for classroom use. Immediately upon the adoption, a controversy ensued between the Twin Lakes School Board and the State Department of Public Instruction. While the controversy waxed hot and the State threatened to cut off school funds for Twin Lakes unless they got rid of the McGuffeys, the newspapers carried daily reports of the skirmishes between the State and the school board.

Meanwhile, the public, reading these daily stories which were prominently featured, began to wonder what the devil the McGuffey Reader was to have caused all this fuss. Some people thought it had something to do with the John Birch Society. Others thought that McGuffey was subtly instilling their children with Protestantism. The general impression was given that in some sort of way McGuffey was controversial. But a large body of readers stoutly defended McGuffey as a darn good reader that would help their kids to learn to read.

While the battle between the educators, now joined by clergymen and teachers, continued to rage, I began receiving a few requests for the readers. I remembered that McGuffey was reprinted by the American Book Company and ordered a few for stock. They were sold quickly.

It occurred to me at this point that if a small ad were placed in the paper, advertising McGuffey, we might sell a few more copies. The first very small ad was one inch. Orders began to trickle in. I repeated the ad several times and orders now continued to come in steadily from all parts of the state. However, it looked as if the controversy was beginning to subside and our sale of McGuffey would consequently collapse, when something unexpected happened. The Milwaukee *Journal* in which paper our ad had appeared phoned me for an interview on how our ads for McGuffey had pulled, and generally what had been our experience with the Reader during the Twin Lakes controversy.

I gave them the following interview, which was published in the Milwaukee *Journal* on Sunday, November 26, 1961:

"The McGuffey Reader controversy has paid off for at least one individual, a bookseller, because of the interest generated in the 19th century school books. 'We had a tremendous sale of them to all parts of the state,' said Harry W. Schwartz, operator of a bookshop on Wisconsin Avenue. 'We never carried them before because there was little call for them.'

"Schwartz said he had sold several hundred of McGuffey's Eclectic Readers. He advertised them for sale after the Twin Lakes (Kenosha County) school board's adoption of them for class room use stirred up a controversy. 'They are being bought by two classes of people,' he said. 'One is the older group who are buying them for nostalgic reasons. The other buys them because they believe they are good books for their children to read. The second group slightly outnumbered the first,' Schwartz said. However, the first group tended to purchase complete sets of the Primer and six Readers, while the second group usually bought one or two books suited to their children's age levels.

"A few sets were purchased by school systems to put into reference libraries. Outside of a book that has been suppressed or banned or something like Henry Miller's *Tropic of Cancer* there has been no specific case of anything like those old books (the McGuffeys) reappearing and becoming best sellers," Schwartz said.

This interview was published in the Milwaukee *Journal* on Sunday, November 26. On Monday morning we usually have a heavy mail, and I didn't receive more than one or two orders for McGuffey. But our phone was busy the entire day answering questions about McGuffey Readers. Our regular customers complained that they were unable to reach us by phone. On Tuesday, Wednesday, and Thursday the orders and inquiries began to flow in. Also the phone kept ringing with a steady stream of inquiries. Of course, not all of these inquiries resulted in sales. Most people just called out of curiosity. Others wanted to learn the price of the Readers, etc. But the climax to all this was yet to come.

The U. P. I. wire service picked up the story of my interview from the Milwaukee *Journal* and under various headings, such as "Big Boom in McGuffeys" or "McGuffey Dispute Aids Book Dealers," etc., printed a condensed version of the interview. And now we were buried under an avalanche of orders and inquiries. This was no longer a state matter but had become a national affair. Orders and inquiries are pouring in from practically every state in the union with emphasis on Florida and California. The letters, mostly written by hand, are often amusing, sometimes pathetic. Many are from older people who have studied the McGuffey Readers when children. Some are just curious to look at the book that caused so much controversy. One old lady of 79 wants a set for her grandchildren. Another grandmother ordered a set for herself and asked in a postscript if I was the Harry Schwartz she knew during the Spanish-American War and whom she has in her 'memory' books (I wouldn't be born for another five years). None of these people have our street address so they simply address the Harry W. Schwartz Booksellers, Milwaukee. One inquiry came all the way from Texas by registered mail. We received several telegrams. We even received one letter from a fellow named McGuffey who owns a motel in California.

The only note to add to this is that my dear wife, who is answering all the letters, fervently hopes that we shall never get into anything like this again. The climax to all this was when the *Catholic Digest* for October 1962 condensed the article written for the *Publishers' Weekly* and we started another round of selling McGuffey. And all this seems to prove that the McGuffey Readers are not dead.

CHAPTER VI

After Love, Book-collecting is the most
exhilarating sport of all. . .

A Book Hunters Holiday
A. S. W. ROSENBACH

When we moved downtown from Downer Avenue in 1937, there were only two bookstores downtown. Of course, two downtown department stores, the Boston Store and Gimbels, had book sections, but as is customary with department stores, these book sections were minimal. Des Forges Bookstore was the oldest bookstore in the city. Although operating under the same name, its ownership had changed hands several times. The second store was owned by the Hampel family and it was somewhat of a political institution. It was a front from which it sold the city all its book requirements as well as all the books for the public library system, a sizable amount. The Milwaukee *Journal* with my help was responsible for exposing this collusion and it was discontinued, with the city hereafter buying its public library needs through a system of bids.

Hampel resented my move downtown and his resentment took an anti-Semitic twist when he asked one of my customers what my name was before I changed it to Schwartz. Downtown for us has really meant W. Wisconsin Avenue and, as explained earlier, our first move downtown was a failure. The rent was cheap and the public library nearby seemed to offer a promise. But it was a near disaster and we learned a sound lesson: a store that needs people has to be located at the hub of pedestrian traffic. So when we moved to Sixth and W.

89

Wisconsin Avenue, although only one block from our old
location, the traffic pattern was radically different and it can
be claimed that our move downtown first commenced with
this second move.

Moving into the new location was a joyous event. We knew
that it had to be better because it could not be worse. Only one
circumstance marred our pleasure: the thought that the
country might soon be at war. As the store was considerably
smaller than the old one I remodeled the basement for our
secondhand books, which I could not bear to relinquish.

As surmised, the new location was excellent. It seemed
difficult to explain how one block eastward could make such
a difference. The emphasis now was on new books and the
secondhand department declined drastically. I continued to
buy libraries but I discontinued my catalogs and sold what I
could locally; what I could not dispose of in the store, I sent
up to auction in New York. However, the new-book business
began to foreclose on the old and more and more of my effort
was devoted to current books.

Also, it became more difficult to obtain private libraries as
more wealthy people began donating them to institutions as
tax losses instead of selling them. A person in a high tax
bracket was allowed, in a new law, to contribute his library (if
he had one) to a public or private institution and deduct the
value of the contribution from his taxes. I reluctantly began to
accept the fact that the old-book business was finished. And
now, in addition to the tax credit for valuable libraries, even
the owners of small collections began to offer them at local
auctions where the prices were surprisingly good. However,
each time I changed locations downtown I moved the old
books along with me, unwilling to give them up. Finally in
1970, preparatory to selling the bookstore and assuming that
the new owners would not want the old books, I sold all my

This was our first downtown store at 723 W. Wisconsin Avenue.

The main floor at 607 W. Wisconsin Avenue.

This was the basement at 607 W. Wisconsin Avenue.
It held our secondhand books.

The main floor at 434 W. Wisconsin Avenue.

Upstairs secondhand department at 434 W. Wisconsin Avenue,
our third move downtown.

440 W. Wisconsin Avenue. Our fourth and present store.

old books en bloc to a California bookseller. It proved to be another of my regrets, like the selling of my Faulkner first-edition collection. I seldom experienced regrets in buying books but almost every time I sold something I immediately was overcome with misgivings.

Now that I turned to new books exclusively, I sought out effective ways of selling them. I observed that none of the bookstores stocked much in the field of scientific or technical books, although Milwaukee was noted for heavy industry manufacture. This puzzled me and I was surprised that all booksellers before my time had ignored such an enormous market. I put in a department of technical books and it did very well. The same was true of business books. When George Bockl published his interesting experiences in Milwaukee real estate we sold several thousand copies. I learned that the only place a student could buy a medical textbook was at the University bookstore. This I was told was very unsatisfactory, because the students were not allowed to examine and compare the books and their prices, which students always enjoy doing. I wrote the medical publishers of my willingness to operate a medical department despite the short discounts. Some of the medical publishers opposed my entering the medical bookselling field. Most medical books are sold by house salesmen who call directly on the doctors and take orders for books that are sent on approval. These books can be returned after ten days' free examination if for any reason they are found unsatisfactory. The medical publishers were worried that I might infringe upon their salesmen's territory and steal their customers. We opened the medical department after we assured the publishers that we would abide by their rules and not interfere with their salesmen. The medical department has done extremely well and today grosses almost $100,000 annually.

This is probably as good a place as any to state what I think of bookselling after having devoted forty-eight years of my life to it. The following is a reprint of an article for the *Publishers' Weekly*, which was published in the issue of February 1, 1960. The article was entitled "Bookselling: One of the Lost Professions."*

The President of the American Booksellers Association was quoted in the *Saturday Review* some months ago as saying that booksellers in America were largely a prosperous group; that bookselling was on the increase; and that the professional could look forward to a flourishing future.

My disagreement is vehement. The truth of the matter is that I consider bookselling one of the lost professions and booksellers very nearly an extinct species. Booksellers, unfortunately, have come to a dead end, and in a few more years will have completely disappeared. They will be a relic of the past, like blacksmithing, but unlike the smithy who was driven out of business by the automobile, the booksellers will have been exterminated largely by the publishers. It may sound strange to some, that publishers, looked upon by most people as the father and mother of booksellers, should actually be the cause of their extinction. Yet it is true that booksellers are the unwanted step-children of the publishers, who have been starving them methodically for years. It is no wonder that booksellers are gradually giving up the ghost and the wonder should be that they have been able to survive so long. In order that there should be no misunderstanding as to what I mean by the term bookseller, let me hasten to define it.

A bookseller is a dedicated person. He is not interested in money as such. Neither is he interested in the usual trappings of money. He is a person driven by a feeling for books. Frequently he is a scholar, more often a student, but always a lover of books. Sometimes he sells books that he likes at no profit to him or even

---

* Reprinted from the February 1, 1960 issue of the *Publishers' Weekly*, published by the R. R. Bowker Co. (after January 1968) a Xerox Corp. Copyright 1960 by R. R. Bowker Co./Xerox Corp.

at a loss; and he gives away books for nothing . . . . He enjoys sharing the love of books with his customers. He is a unique person who finds in bookselling a way of life that gives him pleasure.

Perhaps I had better add what bookselling is not. Bookselling is not selling stationery, office furniture, greeting cards, phonograph records, magazines, gifts, art objects, games, art supplies, etc., etc. Bookselling, as the name should imply, is the selling of books. They can be old books, new books, paper books, rare books, but books they must be.

And you may ask what has happened to the booksellers that were formerly selling only books and why have they gone out of business? There is no doubt that the booksellers have been hurt by the numerous book clubs; however, these blows were not the mortal ones. Years ago American booksellers had to contend with subscription bookselling that, in some cases, was formidable competition. For example, most of the encyclopedias are still sold this way today, and to protect these house-to-house salesmen further, the encyclopedia publishers will not let booksellers handle their sets. Booksellers cannot even take an order for an encyclopedia; orders must be turned over to the house-to-house canvassers and, of course, no discounts or commissions are allowed the booksellers. In some cases a canvasser may slip a bookseller a 5 or 10 dollar bill out of his own commission if the bookseller supplied the lead resulting in the sale.

The largest obstacle in the path of bookselling is the publisher. He is usually a businessman who is concerned primarily with profits, although there are a few publishers left who are sincerely interested in good literature. Most publishers think only in terms of gross, net, subsidiary rights, royalties, overhead, etc., etc. If they ever have another thought, it is an exception to the rule. They are, for the most part, worried about money and taxes.

Publishing is conducted today in almost the same manner it was conducted in the 18th century. In a country where enormous growth and rapid development have changed almost everything, publishing has remained in the fossil stage. The reason for this is that publishers as a class are stubborn, reactionary, secretive, and jealous of each other. Although they are almost exclusively concerned with the business end of publishing, the truth is that they are miserable businessmen.

Just think for a moment of a business that is so chaotic that each publisher has his own discount schedule, which varies from that of every other publisher. Then on top of this, discounts of each individual publisher are changed at will, frequently every few months. Imagine a business that sells at so many discounts that it is not unusual for the entire alphabet to be used to designate the confusing categories. Then think of all the books that are sold directly by the publisher. Very often publishers will sell more books direct to retail customers than are sold by the booksellers. In fact, some publishers prefer to sell direct and would like to cut the bookseller out altogether. They have almost succeeded in doing that, too. Can you conceive of General Motors selling a Buick direct to a retail customer; or General Electric selling a washing machine direct to a housewife? Yet most major American publishers not only willingly sell direct to retail customers but aggressively advertise this fact. Publishers will take full page advertisements in most of the large newspapers and magazines in which they will not only solicit retail business but will also frequently undersell the booksellers. This underselling-the-bookseller trick is accomplished in the case of more than one large publisher by the ruse of forming numerous book clubs. (The book club gimmick seems to be the easiest and, of course, the legal way of underselling booksellers.) He will call one book group THE EXECUTIVE BOOK CLUB and to this group he will offer business books at a discount. Another group he will call the REAL ESTATE BOOK CLUB and to these people he will tout books on real estate, etc., etc. Once he has acquired a name for his mailing list he will use it continuously . . . . In point of fact one of the largest American publishers once boasted to me that he had a retail book list of several million names, and wouldn't miss the booksellers if they all dropped dead.

Another obsolete method of doing business is in the methods of handling the return of unsold books. Instead of having an intelligent, uniform system of handling these "unwanted orphans" some publishers look upon returns as non-existent and they won't permit any returns at all. One large publisher who permitted no returns until quite recently practically ceased selling books through the retail trade. Peculiarly enough, he is the same publisher who said he wouldn't miss the booksellers if they all vanished off the face of the earth. The fact that he is now willingly accepting returns is proof that he is not quite as omnipotent as he thought he was.

Some publishers will accept returns on a sort of private and secret arrangement. The arrangement should not appear in writing and it can be broken whenever the publisher wishes. The bookseller, of course, is helpless in this matter, and his only recourse is not to buy the publishers' books. Some publishers permit returns at certain times of the year, but charge a penalty of 10 percent of the net cost of the books, plus all shipping charges. Other publishers permit the return of overstock without penalty, but are not very happy about this, and demand that booksellers list the date of purchase, the discount, the invoice number, the quantity, the price, etc., etc., of all books returned. If these instructions are not followed to the letter, the books will not be accepted. Other publishers will punish with a penalty if these instructions are not followed precisely.

Digging up all the information to follow these rules takes an enormous amount of the bookseller's time. The publisher hopes to discourage the return of most books. Forced with the necessity of searching for all this information, the bookseller will say "to hell with it" and try to get rid of the books some other way. On top of all this the publishers change their return policies almost as frequently as they change their discounts.

One of the few progressive moves made by the publishers in many years is the advance order arrangement to cut down the need for salesmen. Publishing has become so much of a package business that publishers believe it is unnecessary to employ salesmen to sell books to the booksellers. The reason is that most of the new books are unimportant anyhow; that the largest part, and the most profitable, of a publishers' business is his back list; so why employ a salesman to travel around the country (with travel expenses what they are) to try to sell these new books to the booksellers. It is cheaper to fire the salesmen and send the bookseller a packaged assortment picked by the publisher in

New York and sent to the booksellers throughout the country. To sweeten the package, the publisher allows the bookseller to return unsold books without any strings attached.

This arrangement does make sense, because most of the time the salesmen don't know much about the books they are selling anyway. Few publishers' salesmen read the books they are selling. Often the publishers supply them with scanty information, frequently with the author's name and title of the book; and far too often, what little the salesman does tell you is incorrect and heavily biased. In other words, you will get a canned sales pitch that bears little relation to the need for the book in your bookstore, for your particular community or for your clientele. However, if one shudders at the thought of all these books automatically dumped into his store, there is the consoling feature that he won't have to listen to dozens of salesmen usurping his valuable time, reciting a dull spiel on the merits of a new book. The time released from these buying chores can be devoted to creative bookselling.

If most of these conclusions appear depressing it is no one's fault but the publisher's. He is the one who is forcing the bookseller out of business. For many years the publisher was able to attract intelligent men and women who were eager to go into bookselling for the sheer pleasure of dealing with books, and who were willing to deprive themselves of most of the other pleasures of life. However, with the high cost of operation today, these people are no longer able to set up shop, and consequently few people can afford the luxury of going into a business that offers so little remuneration.

The return of unsold books is one of the most difficult problems confronting the publishers and booksellers. It will not disappear by itself. It must be treated intelligently, with the welfare in mind of both publishers and booksellers. It is an unfortunate part of the publishing business. Because it is both instructive and amusing I print the correspondence I had with the firm of Alfred A. Knopf about the problem of returns and their method of handling it. The firm successfully cut out returns from the booksellers, but it almost succeeded in cutting out Knopf as a publisher also. The correspondence began with a general announcement from Knopf as follows:

June 11, 1954

Dear Bookseller,

Effective August 1st we will inaugurate a new return plan which will apply to all our retail accounts. Books published after August 1st will be returnable only under the provisions of this new plan, but all books published before August 1st will be governed by the terms of our existing arrangement.

The new plan: In January and July of each year you will be authorized to return overstock of any trade titles up to five per cent of your net purchases in the previous six month period as defined below. We will send you a memorandum showing the dollar amount of this five per cent together with instructions, label to cover your shipment and date of deadline. These returns will be credited in full—there will be no service charge.

The January five per cent will be based on our total billings to you from the previous May 1st through October 31st.

The July five per cent will be based on our total billings to you from the previous November 1st through April 30th.

We will send you the first notification of your return allowance under this new plan January next. *Note that this first period will necessarily be based on three months' business only, not six, i.e. August, September and October 1954.*

Books published from November 1st, 1953 through May 31st, 1954 will be returnable in accordance with the old style return list that we will mail you in August.

Books published in June 1, 1954 through July 31st, 1954 will be returnable under an old style return list which we will mail you in November 1954.

Yours faithfully,
Alfred A. Knopf, Inc.

I recognized this threat immediately and replied:

June 24, 1954

Alfred A. Knopf, President
Alfred A. Knopf, Inc.

Dear Mr. Knopf:

I am in receipt of your new return plan, and have just discussed it with your salesman, Leon Anderson, for whom I have high regard.

If you were trying to alienate booksellers from buying your new books you could devise no better method than your new return plan that I have before me. In fact, I am worried that we might reduce our business with your firm so drastically that it might compare with our business with Doubleday when they had a similar plan to that you are inaugurating of 5% returns, some years ago. To give you an idea of what this meant, I am listing the following figures. Last year, our business with Doubleday was about $4300.00, a fairly normal year. When Doubleday had their 5% plan in operation, our business with them was about $300.00.

The Macmillan Co. had a no return of any kind in operation for several years. Our business with them dropped to practically zero. Since last fall they have inaugurated a 100% protection plan and our business with Macmillan is increasing every month.

Our Knopf business is, of course, nothing like our Doubleday business. However, we have always enjoyed selling your books and have felt deep admiration for them and personal enthusiasm, and frequently we have bought books we were aware would be difficult to sell, but we felt, as good booksellers, we should stock them regardless of their potential sale.

I don't believe you will find our returns excessive. However, with your new return plan, it will be practically impossible to stock many of the new books that I have in the past. Some of your books I stocked in ones, twos, and threes because I felt that whereas their sale was limited, as explained above, they were worthy of being displayed, and I felt a bookstore of our type should buy them. However, it is very often that it is these ones, twos and threes we have to return a good proportion of. Based on your present return policy we will have to forego the privilege of stocking most of these books.

I have just finished buying your fall list. If you will take a glance, you will find that I would have liked to have bought almost all of your books. Yet, you will see I was compelled to cut out most of them, in many cases the purchase of which would have been in one, three or five copies.

Mr. Anderson tells me you have had returns from some dealers as high as 40%. I agree with you that this is a terrible return experience. However, I don't think that the method you are employing of limiting your returns to 5% will solve your problem. I am afraid that you will kill the patient instead of offering a remedy.

Sincerely yours,
Harry W. Schwartz

Following my letter to Mr. Knopf I received the following reply:

June 28, 1954

Dear Mr. Schwartz:

I am naturally disappointed by your letter of June 24th, but I am glad to have you express your point of view in detail. I wish I could do something helpful to meet your objections to our new return plan, but I am afraid I cannot. I arrived at it after long and very careful consideration, and while I know that nothing we could do would satisfy all our customers and keep us in business, I believe that our newer arrangements are going to work out on the whole very well indeed.

I hate to do anything to discourage a bookseller like yourself, but I think the usual return arrangement that has become common in recent years is not only fundamentally unsound economically, but in the long run demoralizing and perhaps ruinous for everyone concerned. If in order to keep ours a going business, books have to be sold on a full protection basis or a 90% protection basis, then I am convinced that I am in the wrong business entirely.

However, let's keep an open mind and see what we see.

With best wishes, I am

Yours sincerely,
Alfred A. Knopf

P.S. It seems to me that if you can only do around $4,300.00 with the great firm of Doubleday with all the plain and fancy inducements they make to booksellers to push their stuff, then you ought to be considering seriously working with a good jobber.

When my small order for the Knopf new titles was received the sales manager sent the following unhappy letter:

January 10, 1955

Dear Harry,

If you're sore at us, why don't you say so rather than taking it out on Andy by giving him such a lousy order? I just can't believe you don't find any Knopf books you like any more. What's wrong?

Best always,
William Ashworth
Sales Manager

To which I replied:

Dear Bill,

I was in New York attending a board meeting of the A.B.A. when your letter was received. My secretary sent it on to me at my hotel in New York, but I missed it there so I just got to see it today.

I am not angry at either you or Andy, and I think you are aware of why we are not buying Knopf books the way we did in the past. Your severe restrictions make it impossible to buy your books. We have already gone through this and there is no point to go into it in any further detail, except to say that when you change your return policy, we will again represent Knopf books. Up until that time we are afraid we will have to carry on without you.

The incredible thing about all this is that two large publishers, Macmillan and Doubleday, thought they'd try the same thing, and failed. They needed booksellers much less than Knopf needs them and yet, they came around to the conclusion that they could not stay in the book business without booksellers. Yet, Knopf, who really needs booksellers of my type, is taking their point of view.

Cordially,
Harry W. Schwartz

It required about six months for the firm of Knopf to realize they had made a blunder, because on February 25, 1955 I received the following letter from Knopf's sales manager, Bill Ashworth, with the firm's capitulation.

February 25, 1955

Dear Harry,

I want you to be one of the first to know that effective immediately we have adopted a 100% protection plan for new books. Details follow in a routine way, but I knew you would welcome the good news early.

Cordially,
Bill

February 28, 1955

Dear Customer:

Effective immediately and retroactively to all books published since November 1, 1954, our return plan will be as follows:

All new trade publications may be returned for full credit (under shipping labels to be supplied by us on request) not earlier than six months nor later than one year after their date of publication . . . .

Would you, then, reopen the question of your advance order on our spring list . . . .

Cordially,
Leon S. Anderson

I could not resist "rubbing it in" a little and my letter together with a brief note from Ashworth concludes this strange but typical publisher–bookseller correspondence.

March 3, 1955

Mr. Leon Anderson
Alfred A. Knopf, Inc.

Dear Leon:

I am delighted with your note about the change in your return policy, and have already written to Ashworth about our reaction to it. The letter received from your boss, Alfred A. Knopf, still puzzles me and I would like to have pointed out to him that the last paragraph in this letter,

> If in order to keep ours a going business, books have to be sold on a full protection basis or a 90% protection basis, then I am convinced that I am in the wrong business entirely.

should be written out on a blackboard a thousand times by him in longhand. Or, perhaps, he should be given a dunce's cap and made to sit on a stool in your lavatory for a whole day.

But enough of these gruesome ideas. Please revise the spring order as per the enclosed list. I will be most happy to see you on your next trip.

Cordially,
Harry

March 2, 1955

Dear Harry,

We didn't restore the old plan, we restored better than the old plan. Thanks for writing.

Bill

It seems that survival in the jungle of American business had taken most of my time and energy. And the second threat to survival, although not as severe as the great depression nor of as long duration, for a time appeared disastrous. Because an article I wrote for the *Publishers' Weekly* on March 30, 1964 sums up this near catastrophe, I reprint the piece. The title of the article was "If Discounters Threaten, Don't Panic, Fight Back."*

For the second time in my bookselling career I was confronted by an overwhelming crisis. It was late in 1961 that discounting first hit Milwaukee booksellers and threatened our very existence. Up to this time there had been sporadic price cutting, always by department stores, and generally on the same books. We were accustomed to the kicking around of *The Settlement Cookbook* and *Webster's New World Dictionary* at cut-rate prices. But this discounting of *all* best sellers, fiction and nonfiction, in addition to numerous bread-and-butter books, really frightened me. To obtain a broader knowledge of the extent of this threatened danger I made a trip to the local jobber for the discounters.

I was appalled by what I saw. Here were scores of titles that I sold everyday, and needed to sell in order to pay the rent. There were thousands of books with emphasis on the best sellers and basic stock items. The jobber was placing his books in every department store and shopping center in Milwaukee; he already had 87 outlets and was busily looking for others. As Milwaukee has only six bookshops, most of them small, he was really planning to saturate us with books. I hastened from the warehouse, musing sadly on the low state of the book business.

The first indication of the seriousness of the jobber's threat was large signs placed in the windows of two paperback bookshops one block away from our store, which in large letters read TWENTY PERCENT DISCOUNT ON ALL BEST SELLERS. This was upsetting, but I did not believe it fatal to have two paperback bookstores engage in a little price cutting. After all, I reasoned, wasn't I the best bookseller in town? However, a week

---

* Reprinted from the March 30, 1964 issue of the *Publishers' Weekly,* published by the R. R. Bowker Co. (after January 1968) a Xerox Corp. Copyright 1964 by R. R. Bowker Co./Xerox Corp.

later when I scouted the two big department stores downtown and saw huge signs in the book departments advertising discounting of best sellers, I was shaken. I sought out the buyer of one department store and was told that discounting was introduced only because the management would not be undersold and in order to compete with the shopping centers, books were being discounted as well as some other items. At Gimbels, the biggest department store in our city, I was given the same doleful line of reasoning, which went like this: the buyer informed me "Nobody, but Nobody, Undersells Gimbels."

I wanted to see what books were being discounted at the shopping centers, so I went shopping with my wife to one of our largest supermarkets in a nearby shopping center. Two huge racks were filled with all the latest best sellers, and there were also cookbooks, dictionaries, and even Bibles, plus some children's books. While my wife was shopping I stood with my eyes riveted on the bookracks. And for the first time the thought slammed into my consciousness that probably *I was wrong*, and *this was* the new idea in bookselling; that I was doomed unless I climbed onto the band wagon of discounting, as the manager of the jobbing outfit had warned me. I suddenly felt ill. Was this what I had struggled 36 years for, a discount store?

The next day I held a meeting with my staff to survey the situation and plan our strategy, as the military have it. For we were not only fighting a war but actually a war for survival. To discount or not to discount—that was the question. First of all, we could expect no help from the publishers. I had always viewed publishers as a pusillanimous group and didn't expect much aid from them, but I was hardly prepared for the cynicism with which they approached this new threat to old, established booksellers. My letters to them were almost always answered in the same tone. "Schwartz, legally we can't do anything about it. Our advice, much as we dislike it, is follow suit and discount. There is nothing else to do." Some publishers wrote that discounting was good business, more books would be sold. Others wrote that I was old-fashioned and that I must accept the new idea of discounting, etc., etc. It quickly became obvious that we could expect no help from the publishers. Therefore it was solely up to us. But we were unable to resolve anything, and the meeting adjourned. We felt miserable and defeated.

We now began to notice a falling-off of sales of best sellers. Some days passed without the sale of a single new novel on the best seller list. Also, some of our good charge customers deserted us for the discounters. We felt bitter, lonely, and despairing. Each day I would sneak into one of our large downtown department stores to look at the huge sign posted above the book department, much like the scoreboard in a sports arena. On this sign were the latest best sellers with their list and discount prices, identical with the *New York Times* bestseller list. We held another staff meeting and decided against discounting, but planned how to intensify our efforts to sell more books. We diligently wooed our customers with offers of additional service. We stepped up our advertising. We solicited business from industrial firms and hospitals. We enlarged our display of publishers' remainders, particularly the excellent Bonanza books. We added the wonderful series of cut-out records from Crown Publishers. The addition of these records was indeed a bonanza, and they sold extremely well. We increased our promotion of individual titles that looked like winners.

Example: Last fall we sold more than 400 copies of *Run to Daylight* and we beat the discounters to the punch because we had stock, and they didn't. We ran two cooperative advertisements for this book, and mail orders are still coming in. Example: We sold more than 300 copies of *Birds of Wisconsin* at 18 dollars a copy from two cooperative advertisements, and orders are still coming in. Example: A large store three doors away from us was vacated, and I arranged to use the windows in exchange for keeping them clean and lighted. I filled the windows with Bonanzas and travel posters from Harlem and they have been selling like Beatle wigs.

Surveying the situation over the last two years I can report the following results: The department stores stopped their discounting of books. The shopping centers and supermarkets threw out their books. The paperback bookstores discontinued their discounting of hard back books and returned all their hard back books to the jobber. And, most important of all, the jobber who supplied all these outlets is himself contemplating throwing in the towel. He told me privately that this is the lousiest rat race he has ever been in; that he has consistently lost money on his hard cover operation and that his returns are horrendous. And so what was almost a disaster ended happily, and we are still in the book business and we intend to remain in it.

What moral can be drawn from this episode? Can booksellers in other communities profit from our experience? I believe they can. Discounting as a business method carries within it a fatal germ, at least in bookselling. If you give away one-half of your profit in discounting, you cannot offer the services that your customers want and expect. And bookselling is precisely a business that requires those basic services. It demands someone who is familiar with books and the many tools of the trade. It needs someone who can converse about books and suggest books to be read. It requires someone with imagination, skill and endurance. But above all and indispensable is someone who really loves books and can transfer some of this love of books to a customer. Of course a discounter cannot offer even one of these ingredients that make a successful bookseller, let alone all of them. And so if a discounter threatens you, wherever you are, don't panic, don't run for cover. Take a good sharp look at your store, examine it realistically, and fight back with all the resources at your command.

PART THREE

Of Men and Books

CHAPTER VII

Nothing is more painful to me than the disdain with which people treat
second-rate authors, as if there were room only for the first-raters.

SAINTE-BEUVE

C aspar's Bookstore was more than a bookstore to us. It
was a source of supply, a jobber, a treasure house of first
editions. We browsed there almost daily and seldom did we
come away empty-handed. The prices were ridiculously
cheap, many of the books priced in the 1890s.

The article on Caspar that follows is my tribute to the
Bookstore. It was published in the *Historical Messenger* of
The Milwaukee County Historical Society, Vol. 29, No. 3,
Autumn 1973, and is reprinted by permission.

C. N. CASPAR BOOK EMPORIUM

The C. N. Caspar Book Emporium was a landmark in
Milwaukee and its life span of almost three quarters of a
century made it the "oldest" old bookstore in the city. Carl
Nicolaus Caspar, the founder, was a short stocky man with a
small square beard and an erect military bearing. He dressed
simply, invariably wearing a gray sweater and a black snap-on
bow tie. He always wore a cap in the store. Caspar immigrated
from Germany in 1868 and settled in Cedarburg, Wisconsin.
A little later he became a book salesman for C. Doerflinger of
Milwaukee. It was on one of his selling trips to Indiana that
he found a bookstore closing out its stock of 1,500 old books.
Caspar bought them, moved them to Milwaukee and opened

his bookstore at 35 Oneida Street, now East Wells Street. That was in 1878 and during the next sixty years the store occupied four locations, all within two blocks of each other.

Caspar could not resist a bargain. He thrived on acquiring odd lots of salvaged merchandise, such as books, ink, paper, pencils, greeting cards—in short, anything that was offered cheaply. Caspar would sell enough of the stuff to recover his investment and hoard the balance. When I was asked by the court to inventory the bankrupt bookstore in July 1942, I found valentines that were packed in boxes in 1898 and not opened since. There was enough wrapping paper of different sizes and colors to take care of the store's needs for five hundred years. There were hundreds of bottles of ink that had evaporated and hardened with the years until they resembled bottled coal. There were enough Halloween masks, it appeared, to outfit the entire city. Of course many of these items were spoiled by age or water.

Caspar founded his bookstore at the most auspicious period in Milwaukee's history. The thrifty German Burgher was prospering from his breweries, tanning and other industries and turned his mind toward culture. He bought German books in leather bindings, large paintings of cows and sheep in ornate gilt frames, subsidized a German stock theater and listened to music in a half dozen beer gardens. To supply these customers with books Caspar employed several bookbinders who placed leather bindings on hundreds of sets of Schiller, Goethe, Lessing and dozens of lesser authors, all imported in sheets from Leipzig, the famous German book center. For those who could read French he bound up standard sets of French master-pieces, such as Victor Hugo, de Musset, Balzac, etc. He kept his binders busy turning out these sets, on which he made a nice profit. Caspar engaged in publishing too. In 1889 he published "at a lavish cost of labor and money" a "History of the American Book and Stationery Trade." This was a thick book of 1,400 pages and was praised by "technical critics in both Europe and America." He also published a directory of the "Antiquarian Booksellers in the U. S." in 1885 which was incorporated into the larger book. He published dozens of maps of the city and even German grammars and dictionaries.

The building in which Caspar's was located was a long, narrow, ramshackle affair at 454 East Water Street. The store appeared, at first impression, to be a hodgepodge of books carelessly thrown onto shelves in a helter-skelter manner. Such was not the case at all. If you studied the arrangement for a brief period you began to make sense of the layout. The first floor was largely devoted to new acquisitions and a few new books for which there was a brisk demand at the moment. This was also the floor on which Caspar concealed his erotica, about which there will be more later. It contained the office and bibliographical library, which was impressive. The shelves on this floor reached twenty feet to the ceiling and, of course, books were piled on the floor, on window sills, in doorways, boxes, etc.

The second floor contained fiction. The books were alphabetized and were so numerous that they were double and triple shelved. Caspar never threw out a book; never had a stock reduction sale; never marked a book down. His principle was accumulation and more accumulation. He believed there was a customer for every book in the store; you only had to wait until he showed up. He would much rather lose a sale than take less than the item was marked. "As long as I am living," Caspar is known to have said, "I will do just as I please. I will buy all the books I can. After I am dead they can throw them all out if they want." Today, this floor of fiction would be a gold mine. It is almost impossible to obtain many out-of-print titles of once-popular fiction, and books that Caspar sold for fifty and seventy-five cents would today bring up to five and ten dollars each.

The third floor contained many small rooms of Americana. Sometimes a room was devoted to a single subject. The fourth floor contained Religion and Law and was crowded with periodicals. Caspar did not know the extent of his stock and there was no catalog available. I estimated for the court that there were 250,000 books, although it was only a guess. As the books were marked in code (which I broke in the early months of my going into the book business) customers never knew what price to expect when they finally did search out the book they wanted and brought it downstairs to be priced. The code was JOURNALIST, thus a book marked JNT was one dollar fifty cents. Of course, in a store of this size many books were poorly classified and browsers dragged books to wrong floors and even hid books. When I was appraising the stock I found a rare sixteenth-century Bible hidden in a pile of dust underneath a shelf. One must remember that the building was added to piece by piece (there were no elevators) and the staircases did not always appear in the same locations on the various floors. Some stairs were in the front of the store and others were in the rear, and that is why many browsers were unable to find their way back to the first floor and became lost on the upper floors. Of course, although Caspar's was no Leary's, that great landmark in Philadelphia (now no more), nor a Lowdermilk in Washington, D. C. (also gone), it was a great second-hand bookstore of the kind that no longer exists in America. Even Chicago had nothing to equal it. Moreover, it was an institution that existed on the sale of books alone and acted as a clearinghouse for books for the entire community.

Caspar also dealt in another type of book that, although not as legitimate as his school books and standard sets, nevertheless yielded a juicier profit. This was erotica, or as it is better known today, pornography. Most of these books were quite readily available in France, Germany, Italy, etc., but in America their sale was illegal. Caspar imported these erotic amours from abroad and dispensed them to anyone who could afford the price. I have seen a copy of *Fanny Hill* by John Cleland, one of the most notorious titles of pornography printed by Caspar, thereby suggesting that he found the demand sufficiently great to allow him to dispose of an entire edition. Undoubtedly he sold some copies wholesale to other booksellers. Although I had heard rumors of Caspar's clandestine operations, I never dreamed of the extent of this underground traffic until I stumbled, by chance, upon his private record book. During my inventory I found this innocent-looking battered notebook in a trash bin and placed it in my pocket. I retrieved it only minutes before the trash was dumped into a truck and hauled off to be burned.

Upon examining it later, I found that it contained 130 pages and listed 210 titles of pornography. The first page stated "Those prices marked with violet ink were received after Sept 1st '90." The first 78 pages were English publications; pages 79 to 110 French; and the balance German. The descriptions were concise and three different color inks were used. Violet ink for receipt date; red for price; black for description. Listed also were sources of supply, both domestic and foreign, and both wholesale and retail prices. Also tabulated were the discounts from the selling prices of each supplier.

It was some years later, upon mentioning this private memorandum book to an old local bibliophile, that I was told there existed a large collection of erotica from Caspar's store in the home of a prominent local judge, now deceased. Two maiden aunts inherited the estate and the books, and both were frightened out of their wits upon examining the books. This is the story he told me. (I hesitated to use this story because I was unable to find any substantiating evidence that it was based on fact and not the figment of someone's imagination. But while doing research for this article at the Milwaukee County Historical Society I stumbled on a letter, signed "Fair Play," in which the Comstock story is essentially corroborated. It is a moving plea for Caspar but, much more important, it is the first verification I have discovered of this interesting story and I now feel free to use it.)

The old bibliophile alleged that Caspar had been a thorn in the side of Anthony Comstock, America's greatest vice snooper and implacable enemy of pornography, especially that found in books. Comstock suspected that Caspar was selling erotica but was unable to prove it and could not trap him into a sale. Caspar was careful and only sold for cash and refused to ship except by express. This meant that it was difficult to ensnare the bookseller because shipping by express did not use the U.S. Mail, and consequently he was not vulnerable to Federal prosecution. But of late years, so the old bibliophile continued, Caspar became less cautious. Never having been caught, he began to take chances and even sold the stuff to people he did not know. It was at this time that Comstock baited his trap by sending a money order under an assumed name for a copy of *Fanny Hill, Venus in India* and other well-known titles he suspected that Caspar had in stock. (Unfortunately, the newspaper copy of the letter found in the Historical Society's files is not dated, but checking the watermark we fixed on the dates 1890–95.) With this order was enclosed a letter stating that the writer planned to be in Milwaukee shortly, and if the books were satisfactory he would like to buy and take with him a quantity, because he did not get out often and hated to write letters. This seemed like a plausible reason. Caspar consulted with his chief clerk, who advised against selling the books. However, Caspar was unable to overcome the temptation of the money in hand and sent the books off by express.

Several weeks later a letter arrived at the bookstore stating that the books were satisfactory and setting a date when the writer would be in Milwaukee. On the appointed date Comstock entered the store and asked for Caspar. He introduced himself, said he was eager to see some erotica and didn't have much time. Now it seems that Caspar had a hidden sliding door closet that contained all his pornography. No customers were allowed into this closet, but Comstock appeared to be a man of substantial means and Caspar had visions of a sale running into four figures. Consequently he invited him in and Comstock uncovered one of the largest stocks of pornography in the Midwest.

Comstock made a few selections, paid for them with marked money and, with the excuse of an urgent appointment, left. Shortly after, he returned with a U. S. Marshal and placed Caspar under arrest. The news of the arrest was sensational, for Caspar was a well-known merchant and many of the city's leading citizens were among his customers. Moreover, it was rumored, some of these leading citizens had purchased pornography from Caspar at one time or another. (Maybe this is one of the reasons why it is so difficult to unearth any material on this episode. There is no mention of this story in the excellent biography of Anthony Comstock by Heywood Broun and Margaret Leech, N. Y. 1927.) Caspar's attorneys decided to use entrapment for their defense, but the case looked hopeless for the bookseller. At the trial a huge table was piled with the pornography seized from the bookstore. Comstock obtained an easy conviction. Caspar received a fine and a suspended sentence. The evidence was allegedly destroyed, the old bibliophile winked at me, but the books mysteriously turned up in the Judge's house, and these are the books that are plaguing the maiden aunts.

Lest I've led the reader to believe that Caspar was just an eccentric business man let me quickly add that the old dog had a gay side to him. The bookstore, as stated earlier, occupied a narrow building next door to a run-down hotel called the St. Charles, which for years before it was finally demolished catered to chorus girls and generally shady characters. It was rumored that Caspar outfitted a room on the third floor of his bookstore in which he entertained the lively ladies from the hotel next door. They entered at night through the rear of the store and ascended the back stairs to the cozy hideaway on the third floor. This room was always locked. It was, again, rumored that once or twice when employees worked late they heard women's voices emanating from the secret room. No one had ever seen a woman coming from or going into the room. However, I can attest to the room, which I examined when I was taking inventory. And it could conceivably have made an elegant little bordello.

There is another amusing story told about a fire at Caspar's at the end of the century. Caspar was on one of the upper floors at the time, and learning that fire had started in the basement, he hastened down the ramshackle stairway and found a roaring fire. To his consternation he observed several employees attempting to retrieve the burning books. He yelled at them to throw more books on the fire instead of trying to save them. The books were worth more for their insurance value. The apocryphal story claims that Caspar collected a fair sum for thousands of worthless school books partly burned or water-soaked.

As long as the old man lived the store managed to survive, although its heyday had long since passed. But when he died and the store was bought by an old employee and his son-in-law, its rapid decline commenced. An attempt was made to catalog some of the stock but it was not continued. There was no plan to advertise or to encourage customers to browse in the endless stacks. The partners milked the business steadily and finally the inevitable occurred. When the rent and taxes fell in arrears the store was thrown into bankruptcy. The value of the stock of approximately 250,000 books was appraised at $4,000, while the other assets were fixed at $1,150. Debts were figured at $10,341. On the day of the public sale, which was extensively advertised by the trustees, it seemed that the entire literate population of Milwaukee was there. On the opening of the doors the crowds stretched several blocks. Police let in only a few at a time after the first big rush filled the store. Of course, many of them were curiosity seekers and had no intention of buying any books. But others brought shopping bags, boxes and suitcases and jammed the bargains into them. The valentines and greeting cards were quickly sold. Many of them irreplaceable and valuable, dating back to the nineteenth century, were trampled under foot by the hordes of people.

The referee had brought the sale to the attention of most of the parochial schools in the state. The sisters and priests bought thousands of old school books such as grammars and dictionaries and readers in Latin and Greek, etc. As sections of shelving became denuded on the first floor, employees brought down arms full from the upper floors. Meanwhile, crowds were milling around on the upper floors, many of them lost and trying to puzzle their way down. Of course, hundreds of books were crushed and kicked about; hundreds more were stolen. It was bedlam. Although the public sale disposed of most of the books, a great many remained to be sold. The court decided on an auction to get rid of the balance. I attended the sale. The prices were ridiculously low, many bundles going for ten cents a piece. As I looked around at the empty shelves and dirty walls I seemed to hear the prophetic words that were attributed to Caspar: "As long as I am living I will do just as I please. I will buy all the books I can. After I am dead they can throw them all out if they want."

CHAPTER VIII

I do not know any reading more easy, more fascinating,
more delightful than a catalogue.

Crime of Sylvestre Bonnard
ANATOLE FRANCE

PREFACES

A lthough I issued my catalogs of first editions year after
year, the sale of books fell off dramatically during the
depression years. In an attempt to increase the interest in my
catalogs I thought it would be a good idea to ask some of the
younger writers who were just starting to be collected to write
a preface to them. In many instances I was one of the first
dealers to catalog these authors, and it gave me a great deal of
pleasure to bring them to the attention of my customers. I
have always been interested in younger, unknown writers and
urged my customers to buy and collect them. In this way I
began to sell a few books by H. E. Bates, Rhys Davies, Vardis
Fisher, Robert Nathan, etc., etc. This was, of course, many
years before they became well known and widely collected.

Because these prefaces are so excellent, and because they
explain what an author thinks about first editions and being
collected, I reprint four of them here. So far as I know, this is
the first time they have been reprinted. The four are by H. E.
Bates, Rhys Davies, Vardis Fisher and Robert Nathan.

FIRST EDITIONS WITH A PREFACE
BY H. E. BATES

From time to time, though less frequently than in the past,
an English author receives from America a batch of letters all

bearing the postmark of the same vicinity. They are invariably beautifully typewritten, the paper and envelopes bear collegiate arms, and the signatures are those of students. More than half of them are written by young ladies. Their contents vary from requests for autographs (for which a blank card is enclosed) to verbose requests, almost demands, for the author to give his reasons for believing in God or Mohammed or the efficacy of private prayer. The author, if he is vain, and all authors are, concludes that some distant Kentuckian campus has resounded with his name or that the state of Virginia has come to the conclusion that he is one with Shakespeare. If he is a fool, and all authors are, he scribbles out his signature, expounds his views on God and morality or whatever it is, at length; tells the Virginians that he reciprocates their tender feelings and sits down and waits for results. The result never comes. He concludes that Americans are ungrateful devils and resolves that he will never again waste a signature on an American, and keeps that resolve as long as there are no letters from Illinois or Massachusetts to praise his name. When they arrive his vanity succumbs again.

It took me a long time to realize that these letters were meant to be something more than sop food for my vanity. It was not until the banking crisis of 1931, when such letters ceased abruptly altogether, that I realized that they had an economic significance, and that what I had regarded as many expressions of Americans' regard for me were in fact nothing more than manifestations of This Book Collecting Racket. In short, I had been fooled. I had been distributing my signature over the face of America with a prodigality that seemed more idiotic every time I thought about it. And I saw that for me it was a losing game, whatever it was for the students of Virginia. For apart from the fact that I was rarely, if ever, thanked for my pains, my books continued to be unread by Americans, my publishers in New York succeeded each other in rapid bankruptcy or in a feverish desire to throw Bates, the literary Jonah, overboard, and no single American editor, until Mr. Whit Burnett came to my rescue, would trouble to print my stories in his pages. I saw clearly that I was a damn fool.

But now when I reflect on it, I hardly think I was a bigger damn fool than the students of Virginia. For though I never received a penny for my trouble I certainly hadn't invested a penny which I could lose, whereas it was obvious that the Virginians had invested a good deal in me and my future as a writer. What the Virginians banked on were two things: my doubling in value of their first editions by adding my autograph, and my writing a second *Anna Karenina* or its equivalent, so that they might receive in return for the original five dollars they had paid for a first edition of *The Two Sisters*, a hundred dollars or a thousand, just as they knew people had done in the same way with Conrad's *Chance*.

What I don't think the Virginians, and by that I mean all young American collectors, understood were the economics of the game. I believe all of them hoped that in time there would be only one copy of *The Two Sisters* left in the world, and that their own. They did not trouble to consider that originally there had been issued 1,500 copies of that book and perhaps 50 of that number were still reposing, unsoiled and perhaps unread, in the sacred book rooms of all good book collectors on both sides of the Atlantic. The chance of *The Two Sisters* becoming a rarity was, in short, pretty rotten, and the only remedy the Virginians had by this time, apart from kicking themselves, was to throw their copies of my first novel down the nearest drain.

There is just one among all those collectors who has no cause to kick himself. And he is the small English bookseller who, in 1927, bought the 400-page MS. of *The Two Sisters* at just about twice the price the Virginians paid for their copies of this book. He has no cause for regret and possibly never will have. For he began at the point where most collectors hope to come off, secure in the knowledge that his MS. was the only one in the world, and that there never will be another. However he regarded it, that MS. was a good investment, for if posterity decided that I was a bad egg he could still keep the story as a piece of literary curiosity, a relic of the age when authors wrote their novels with pens instead of typewriters.

All of which brings me to the point of these remarks: that the young collector, if he wishes to revive his faith in collecting, should explore the possibilities of MSS. He will find it an infinitely more exciting and, I believe in the end, profitable pursuit than the indiscriminate hoarding of precocious work on hand-made paper. If he doubts my word as to the profits of this business let him consider for a moment the difference between the prices fetched by first editions of Dickens and the price paid for MS. sheets of *Pickwick Papers.* It is obvious that the student-collector will not hope to acquire the MSS. of such English authors as Coppard, Davies, Manhood, O'Flaherty, O'Faelain and others for surprisingly modest sums. For myself I may say that I have repeatedly sold MSS. of stories for very little more than the price asked for a first edition of my novels. And of three stories there was only one copy and there will never be another.

All this may appear to be something of a backhander to Mr. Schwartz. But it is very obvious that Schwartz will begin to stock MSS. as soon as his customers demand it, just as he has been stocking first editions. And I look forward to the day when he will be issuing, not a catalog of first editions, which even he with all his originality cannot make unique, but a catalog of MSS. I should begin to believe then that Americans are not such fools as I sometimes think them now.

FIRST EDITIONS WITH A PREFACE
BY RHYS DAVIES

"Sir, you write well, but you shame the mother who bore you." Thus an anonymous person began a postcard to me recently. Nowadays, to me, the opinion of members of the reading public is of more interest than that of the professional reviewers. I like a whinny of pleasure—or a snort of anger—straight from the horse's mouth, as it were. But particularly I like receiving abuse through the post, and out of letters from strangers it is the insulting ones that I keep, pleasing though it is to receive those charming notes of appreciation which make one eat a breakfast with more ardor than usual. And since the letters I receive from America are always pleasant I thought it would be of interest to tell you what one or two of my British readers think.

A treasured letter is one sent me by a lady (not anonymous too) from a farm in Berkshire, and now and again when I feel liverishly that compared with life all literature is bogus and not worthwhile, I take it out to refreshen me. There are eight pages and I regret that I cannot quote all this lady's abuse. First she petitions me not to inflict on a long-suffering public stories based "No doubt on your own disgusting married life." With gathering fury, she goes on, "Is it too much to ask men to respect the modesty of women who do not want their (rose-white) or any other colored bellies referred to in public print? Kindly confine yourself to your so-called wife's belly and do not strip all women in public." After accusing me of all manner of "sport" in my private life, she shouts, "Write about your own blasted belly for a change." And she is sick of "blasted male novelists writing about women's private parts in public."

This letter caused the bacon on my plate to become cold. I read it again and again. No whoop of joy broke from me. But

I felt deeply honored and deeply grateful to this lady, shouting at me from the furious, breakneck scrawl of the letter. What were the dingy laurels of long "interesting" newspaper reviews, compared to this vital wrath. My stories had done their trick. They had obviously stung a reader out of her chair, had whipped up her mind. (Though indeed that mind may be a very queer one . . . . And anyone reading her letter might think that the anatomical parts she mentions are scattered all over my books ... a gross untruth?)

Then there was that man in Newquay, Cornwall—but on rereading his letter I find its rudeness pedantic and literary, dull. And there was the Welshman who called me (on a postcard) a "lousy fox in sheep's clothing." A young girl of 19 (so she says) from Shropshire exclaims derisively that, my God, a woman must have done "something to me," but she relents at the end of her letter and praises me for writing of the pleasures obtained from what she calls "the movement of the bowels."

This little preface which Mr. Schwartz asked me to write for his catalog is not, however, an invitation to his first edition collectors to send me long, flattering letters of abuse. Oh no, I have, in spite of what I've written, a secret fear that if I receive too many assaults I might be battered out of existence. Honeyed praise and sweet sounding tinkles of appreciation are, after all, the quickest shortcut to that blessed fairyland where books sell like hot cakes. Or at least it seems so.

FIRST EDITIONS WITH A PREFACE
BY VARDIS FISHER

Perhaps nothing in this country today is quite so precarious as a literary reputation. Because publishers have to be specialists in ballyhoo, authors who flash like a rocket in one year often discover, in the next, that they were buried under superlatives. It is, indeed, no small handicap nowadays to discover that you have written the great American Novel; or, having missed such a catastrophe, to learn that you are standing where some immortal once stood. In either case you are expected, on your next attempt, to bring American Literature to its final smashing climax.

Such disaster has not, most fortunately, overtaken me yet. But there are other oblivions awaiting the writer, particularly if his work has individuality of its own. If he devotes his pages to half-wittedness or incest or to any other subject that has not been exploited, he is at once trademarked, quite as if he were a breakfast food; and he is regarded as a traitor if, weary of incest, he tries his hand at roses and moonlight. Because this is a country of trademarks; and books are a commodity, like gasoline and coffee; and it seems no more reasonable to the public for a gloomy author to become happy than for Conoco Bronze to pretend to be a cocktail syrup.

And here am I, alas, being an established writer, against my will, under the aegis of the word brutal. In despair I look around me and see reports of lynching and Jew-baitings, rapine and third-degrees, which make my novels read like Sunday School fables. Never, I reflect, have I been able to approach the cruelty recorded in the Bible; nor the torture of humanity by humanity which has given color and distinction to history everywhere. I reflect, too, that those who find my books so brutal as most likely repressing a strong sadistic lust; and so condemn me that they may feel more at peace with themselves. But such reflections do not help me at all. There is so much more that I want to write of besides what some are pleased to call brutality. I don't want to be retired to what some are already calling my Antelope Wesses.

As a matter of fact, my books, save possibly Bridwell, are not tragedies. They are, in plain truth, high comedy; because they show persons chastened or defeated by an assumption of virtue entirely in excess of what human beings have. But the symbols of tragedy, as established in our tradition and folklore, are the symbols, it would seem, of frustrated vanity and stupidity, and not of that fate which, anciently and today, still often reduce us to humiliation in which our vanity played no significant part. Of my books it is apparently asked, does anyone suffer? Does anyone fail to get what he wants? If so, then damn it, your books are tragedies! And there you have it.

If I am footnoted in a history of American literature, the appraisal, I can easily imagine, may take this solemn declaration:

Vardis Fisher, as gloomy and morbid a person as ever brooded over Dostoevski, or invited Leopardi to maneuver his dreams, was a belated offshoot of that sober and terrifying earnestness which was midwife and mother to Zola and Dreiser. His hatred was savage and, in some respects, painstaking. He seemed to fancy himself in possession of a first mortgage on everything horrible; and with blundering zeal he strove, in book after book, to foreclose the mortgage. Without any sense of humor at all, and with no perspective on the unfortunate years which have left him bitter and jaundiced, he sipped his aconite and pounded his typewriter; and time in its charitable way is now restoring his books to that darkness out of which they came—and I protest. But so, doubtless, did many others.

FIRST EDITIONS WITH A PREFACE
BY ROBERT NATHAN

When I was a little boy, I was always told not to bite the hand that fed me. The memory of that not unreasonable request would deter me now, were I not too well aware that the hand which collects the first editions of my books, feeds me not at all. It is true that twice in the last fifteen years, I have received some bits of food from friendly readers; once a cookie baked in the form of my little dog Musket, and once a whole box of little cakes. But those were the exceptions.

Among the curious things about the collecting of first editions, is the fact that the collector does not help his favorite author to live. The book which is sold for $52.35 three years after its publication (I am not speaking of my own) brought to its happy creator only his original 30 cents in royalties. As a matter of fact, it is not at all unlikely that the author's death, from neglect or starvation, would even increase the value of his books to the collector. I have no quarrel with this plan; I merely mention it. It is part of the divine economy of the world. It is equally true for the painters and for countries which issue stamps.

I suppose there is no profession in the world which makes more use of Amateurism than the profession of collecting. Because, in general, only those things are collected which were never brought into the world for that purpose. The true passion is not for the elegantly prepared "Collector's item"; it is for the brown, unnoticeable little book with a word misspelt on page three, and the words "first published in" or no words at all in front.

It is for such reasons as these that the author can do no business in his own first editions. If he were to collect them himself, the market would take fright, and dash away from him. It would lack that sense of the unexpected, the unforeseen, which more than anything else distinguishes its victories.

Yes, the author must be indifferent, he must stand to gain nothing; it must all be an accident. Therefore, by accident, I am in these pages, along with men and women from I to P. It was also not unforeseen that I would have very little to say for myself, if I were called upon to write a preface to the catalog. But that does not seem to me so much of an accident as the other.

CHAPTER IX

By far the most widespread and tenacious characteristic of
man is hypocrisy and dissimulation.

MAX NORDAU

TRAVEN

I have made it a lifelong rule not to visit an author or to
seek to know him other than through his books. I have
always believed that I would rather cherish my illusions of an
author than see him in the naked flesh. I have already written
of my interrupted journey to visit Vardis Fisher. I do not believe I have mentioned my trip through Oxford, Mississippi,
the home of William Faulkner.

It was the summer of 1956 and we were returning from a
vacation in New Orleans. As we entered Mississippi my wife
remarked that we would pass about 50 miles from Oxford, and
we should stop and say hello to Faulkner. We had published a
collection of Faulkner called *Salmagundi* twenty-five years
earlier and I had one of the largest personal collections of first
editions of Faulkner in private hands. I also believed that he
was one of the greatest living writers of prose. However, I did
not believe that all this awareness of his genius gave me the
privilege of breaking in on him to say hello, just because I was
driving through Mississippi on my way home from a vacation.

These were some of the thoughts I pondered when my wife
and I planned our vacation in Mexico City. Of course we would
have to visit Traven. Now perhaps some people still do not know
who Traven was. I will just say here that he was one of the greatest

131

writers of the century. (Traven died March 26, 1969.) Six of his
books have recently been reprinted. Because what I have written
about Traven in *This Book Collecting Racket* published thirty
years ago still remains valid to this day, I quote from it:

> There is one American writer who is almost unknown in
> America, yet whose books have sold over 2,000,000 copies in
> the fourteen countries in which they have been published. Not
> only are his books practically unknown in his own country, but
> the author himself is a legendary figure and some critics even
> deny he is an American. One critic claims he is a German whose
> books are translated into English; another believes he is an
> Englishman; while he has been called variously a Russian, a
> Slav, a Spaniard and a Mexican.
>
> If he is an American, his only rival for European popularity
> is Jack London, while in America his publishers report that of a
> first edition of 2,200 copies of his best known work *The Death
> Ship*, few copies have been sold. You may have already guessed
> that this strange writer is B. Traven. His books are, in order of
> their publication: *The Death Ship*, New York 1934; *The Treasure
> of the Sierra Madre*, London 1934; *Caretta*, London 1935;
> *Government*, London 1935. To further complicate matters we
> find that the London edition of *The Death Ship* was a translation,
> while the Knopf edition was printed from the manuscript. The
> London *Treasure of the Sierra Madre*, which preceded the New
> York edition, was also a translation, while the Knopf edition was
> printed from the manuscript. *Government* is a translation, but
> *Caretta* apparently is not.
>
> Traven's peculiarities do not end here. When Mr. Knopf first
> approached him he refused to have anything to do with America.
> Later, however, he relented to the extent of permitting his
> celebrated *Death Ship* to appear. The publisher, nonetheless, was
> compelled to comply with the following odd conditions: there
> was to be no advertising, or at least very little; there was to be
> no blurb of any sort on the wrapper; the few copies sold, to start
> with, the better Mr. Traven would like it. Surely strange condi-
> tions for an author to demand.
>
> I might add that *The Death Ship* and *The Treasure of the
> Sierra Madre* are as adventurous and exciting as any two books

you can mention. But they are more than adventure stories. They are filled with a varied and amazing knowledge; they indicate an understanding and sympathy for the downtrodden that few writers possess; they make use of a philosophic wisdom such as you seldom encounter in fiction; and last, but not least, they are packed with social dynamite.

I sent a copy of *This Book Collecting Racket* to Traven in 1937, who replied with a most revealing letter from which I quote: "May I just mention that my first name is not Bruno, of course not; neither is it Ben nor Benno. These names, like the many nationalities I have, among them the German, are inventions of critics who want to be smart and well informed. Several times I have protested in European publications that I am not even of German race or blood. The publishers of the German editions of my books knew from the first day of our relations that I am an American, born in the U.S.A. Why my books were published in Europe and not in this country first is another story. You are right in saying that only a few copies of my books, so far, have been sold in the U.S.A. Recently a Slovakian edition of one of my books (*Sonnen-Schoffung*) was published in Bratislava. Sorry, I can't find this town on the map, but the book sold, in this edition, twelve hundred copies inside of six weeks. We needed more than six months to sell the same amount of copies of the same book in this country, the native country of the author, which you can find on any map no matter how small."

Our trip to Mexico City started in May 1967 with our flight to San Francisco, then to Ensenada, Mexico to visit friends, and on to Mexico City. I had written Traven hopefully asking for an appointment, but our departure was so sudden that there was barely time to receive a reply. I had asked him to reply to the St. Francis Hotel in San Francisco, or to my friends in Ensenada. On our last day in San Francisco we received a letter asking us to call when we arrived in Mexico City. When we arrived in Ensenada we received a second letter thoughtfully sent in case the first letter bypassed us.

In Mexico City I called Traven, and we received an appointment for the following day. My hotel telephone rang on the afternoon of our appointment and for a moment I feared that our meeting was to be postponed. However, it was Traven's wife-secretary, R. E. Lujan, telling me that she would pick us up at the hotel at 4 P.M. She would be driving a white Chevelle and we should be at the curb. Knowing how difficult it was to see Traven and how many people had attempted to interview him and failed, I was still skeptical of my good fortune. One of the side purposes of our trip was to allow me to examine his library, which he had proposed to sell. The sale of his library was complicated by his offers to several University libraries, particularly to Texas, Yale and the Newberry.

Promptly at 4 P.M. a white Chevelle stopped at the curb, driven by a handsome woman who, of course, was Mrs. Lujan. She immediately took us to their home, one of several they owned in Mexico. The other is a ranch where Traven provided a home for fifty-six dogs. This house in the city was a modest three-story dwelling, with an enclosed garden in the rear in which two dogs were romping. Coming into the house we entered the library, a narrow room with bookshelves from floor to ceiling. In a few moments Mrs. Traven went upstairs to fetch her husband, who was working in his study. Traven was a frail man of medium height who looked all of his seventy-seven years. His hair was white. He grudgingly used a hearing aid, which he detested. His glasses were fitted with extremely heavy lenses and he talked in a faltering English. His wife explained that they seldom talked in English but spoke mostly Spanish. Traven wrote in English, Spanish and German.

I asked him why he wrote *The Rebellion of the Hanged* in Spanish and had it translated into English, instead of writing it in English in the first place. This question was not answered. When I first began to read *The Death Ship* I was struck by the many instances of German language syntax. This was long before I learned of the possibility of Traven being Ret Marut. There was something unconvincing about the American language. Although, at the time, I did not have the help of Baumann's "B. Traven, An Introduction," I suspected that Traven's English was German in origin.

I will not immerse the reader in the Marut–Traven controversy; readers can turn to Baumann for that. I will merely state that the quality of Traven's English retained the strong German bias that would be natural after having written in German for many years. As Baumann states on pages 87–88: "He had chosen early in the 1900s to express himself in German and his relatively infrequent attempts to write in English for his American publishers were simply not fated to be successful."

According to Charles H. Miller, Traven's friend and bibliographer, Traven's full name is Traven Torsvan, born in Chicago in 1890. His parents were named Burton and Dorothy Torsvan, Norwegian-Swedish immigrants. I gather the impression that what I saw was only the shell of a man who in his earlier years was a robust and vital person. His wife is also his secretary and translator. Traven had been in poor health for some time. He required a hernia operation but had resisted having it done. His wife was trying to convince him of the necessity. His mind seemed alert, and although his poor hearing enabled him to take only a small part in the conversation, whenever he did reply to a question (talked into his ear by his wife) his response was spirited. His pale blue eyes behind their thick lenses came to life occasionally. When I mentioned his motion pictures he insisted (against his wife's wish) on climbing the stairs and bringing down several film posters for the motion picture "The Death Ship," produced in Germany after a great deal of squabbling. Traven said that the producer insisted, against his opposition, on putting a woman in the story, although, of course, no woman appears in the book. It seems that all of Traven's motion pictures ended in controversy or suppression.

An American film classic was produced from *The Treasure of the Sierra Madre*. The great film "Macario," made from the famous short story, was suppressed by the Mexican government. It had won ten international film awards. In 1961 "Rosa Blanca" was released as an important film produced under a record Mexican budget, but was withdrawn due to diplomatic complaints of its controversial nature. Other films have been made from *The Rebellion of the Hanged, Canastitas* (Bush Stories) and *Autumn Days*. A film is being made from *Night Visitor*.

The library was filled with translations of his books, which appeared in over thirty languages, including Hindu, Chinese and Russian. Traven managed to have at least three copies of each translation, although in many cases there were at least half a dozen. On the walls of the hall leading to the living room were many paintings, and one portrait of Traven was particularly striking. It revealed him considerably younger with a full head of blond hair and strong Scandinavian features.

It would be incorrect to call this an interview, and I was reluctant to press many questions. I simply let him do the talking. The people that have been allowed to see Traven could probably be counted on the fingers of both hands. I realized that I was being accorded a great privilege. Following tea and cookies (baked by Mrs. Traven) Mrs. Traven took command of the conversation and told us of her two daughters, one of whom was studying at the Sorbonne in Paris. We talked about Traven's books; she also told us many things about Mexico City that are not in the guidebooks. Our visit lasted about three hours and I could detect that Traven was tiring. He turned to me and said, "Mr. Schwartz, it is a great privilege to have you visit us." It was unbelievable that this famous writer could consider it a privilege to have me, an obscure bookseller, visit him. I felt very humble, as we shook hands and he asked with a sparkle in his eye, "Tell me, Mr. Schwartz, is book collecting still a racket?" And he turned to my wife and said with a gallant bow, "And I am not too old a caballero to deem it a privilege to kiss a lady's hand."

In the weeks that followed this visit with Traven, I reread his *The Death Ship, Bridge in the Jungle, The Treasure of the Sierra Madre,* and *The Rebellion of the Hanged.* I wanted to determine how the stories would endure, since I had read them almost thirty years ago. I found that *Treasure* was still a fascinating story, while *Bridge* dragged. *Rebellion* seemed even better the second time. What makes Traven's stories exciting? I believe it is, first, his superb ability to etch the jungle. You are suffocated with the stench of the swamps in *Rebellion.* The Indians are perhaps too heroic, but only because they are put into juxtaposition with the white owners. The cruelty inflicted upon the Indians is almost unbelievable. One must remember that many of these stories are laid in Mexico before the Revolution and the fall of the Diaz dictatorship. Also, in *Rebellion,* Don Felix, Don Severo and Don Acacio are monsters indistinguishable one from the other. In a similar way the Indians are presented en masse as martyrs, without a single individual character created among them. It is this lack of convincing characters that weaken Traven's stories. The background of the implacable jungle is fascinating; the knowledge of history, economics and psychology of the Indian is formidable. Yet with all this there is no fashioning of a single Indian character.

Although there are no plausible Indians, it is the knowledge of Indian mode of living that Traven uses to such good advantage. Not only does he have a solid knowledge of the jungle, but he knows its inhabitants equally as well. Yet in spite of all the Indians he has described in his stories, none of them appears as a fully developed character. As an example, Dobbs in *Treasure* becomes a living human being, created of flesh and blood. He is despicable but believable. Howard, on the other hand, is idealized out of existence and in the process becomes a prop on which to hang the story. The philosophy of Traven is a kind of Anarchism. It is carefully to be distinguished from Communism, of which he is sharply critical. He is against any kind of exploitation of one man by another. He paints Capitalism in harsh terms and the Capitalist System is held up to ridicule. He looks on the world as a place infested by monsters like the Montellano brothers (in *The Rebellion of the Hanged*). On the other hand, he sees the Indians who are continually being pursued by the Montellano as primitive, naive and dignified. To make it easier for the Montellano to exploit the Indians, he presents them as children who believe in the power of Destiny, from which it is impossible for them to escape. They are caught in a trap. As Traven states it on page 7 of *The Rebellion of the Hanged*:

> In the depths of his soul the Indian believes more in the power of destiny than in that of any God whatever. He knows that, do what he may, he cannot escape that destiny. When he sees its approach, the Indian comports himself like all human beings; the purely biological instinct of self-preservation drives him to resist by all available means, by whatever methods he imagines can help him, including invocation to the Saints . . . who can communicate, as every one knows, with God. But he understands perfectly that he is like a lost sentinel, and that if he opposes his destiny, it is merely to delay its action a little.

This explains why a handful of Spaniards under Cortez's leadership were able to overcome Montezuma and his well-trained army. Montezuma believed that Cortez was a God, and that it was Montezuma's destiny to be destroyed by this God. Therefore, Montezuma yielded his impregnable city and even protected the Conquistadors until his own death let loose the opposing forces which he alone had held in check.

When Traven writes of the Establishment he implies dishonesty, graft and corruption. The Police are venal and brutal. (Of course all this is pre-revolution.) It is the primitive, hardworking and suffering Indian who is the folk hero of most of his stories. In attacking the church, Traven is subtle and ironic. However, the church is presented as corrupt. Individual fathers of the church may indeed be delineated as honest and well-wishing, but they are also shown as helpless pawns held imprisoned by the power structure of Mother Church. Confronted with these overwhelming odds, the Indian is indeed helpless. By nature ignorant and superstitious he is easily persuaded that he cannot escape these evils. He is aware that the Church and the Government support the Montellano and he feels himself helpless. It is his Destiny.

Such is the background of many of Traven's stories, and under these circumstances many of the stories unfold. The stories acquire the pattern of Greek Tragedy and inexorably unravel the foreordained plots. What follows is sad and inevitably cruel. Traven implies that life could be pleasant, even joyful, were it not for these jackals in the guise of the Montellano, the Church and the Government. Cannot the Indian escape? Where to? His country is firmly in the grasp of the unholy triumvirate. Should he be lucky enough to escape one, he will surely fall into a trap of the other. They are always lurking for him wherever he might be.

In *The Death Ship* one is confronted with the type of outcast that Traven loves to write about. This quotation from page 34 of *The Death Ship* will set the theme of the story: "A civilized country means a country that sends to jail a man found asleep in the streets without evening clothes. You have to have a house or at least a room to sleep in. How you get it is of no concern to the police." It is possible that Traven borrowed this from that master of irony, Anatole France, whose phrase is, "In the majesty of the Law both the rich and the poor can sleep under the bridge...." The sailor of the story is followed through an endless series of cruel experiences, one more savage than the other. This book illustrates superbly man's inhumanity to man. In fact, in the entire story there emerges only one decent human being.

Traven believes that man could be decent but the system makes him a villain, or in the words of Bertold Brecht, another brilliant critic of the system, "It's circumstances that makes him so." Even when he strives to be sympathetic he is immediately frightened back into his villainy. Capitalism has so corrupted him that he has forgotten that he ever was a man. And this includes the Fascists and Communists. On page 99 of *The Death Ship* he states, "The Communists in Russia are no less despotic than the Fascists in Italy or the Textile mill owner in America." Are there then no decent characters in Traven's books? No. That is perhaps a weakness and the stories would be more persuasive if there were a few. On the other hand, the strength of Traven's books consists particularly in his knowledge of human weakness, depravity and general odiousness. He permits thin remnants of decency to emerge under the hardened shell of malevolence. In *The Death Ship*, for instance, the American Consul would like to do something decent but is prevented from doing it by the many years of bureaucratic hypocrisy he has spent in the consular service.

There are many individual policemen, ships officers, civil servants, even judges who could be sympathetic human beings but they are unable to respond because of their training.

The jungle of capitalism has made of man something resembling a beast. It is survival of the fittest, with the stronger destroying the weaker in this human jungle. It is true that there are a few people in the world who are aware that they are human, but they are mostly found among the failures and outcasts of society. These are the brave and courageous ones who the system has destroyed because they stubbornly refused to surrender. Because they refused to accept the values of deceit, hypocrisy and the innumerable forms of chicanery and venery our society consists of, they have been pursued relentlessly and destroyed.

There are few women in Traven's stories. One can assume that if there were women in his stories, they too would be knocked about the same as his men. The Jungle, whether of the kind found in the interior of Mexico or in any of the large cities of the world, does not respect the female any more than the male of the species. And quite naturally, the few women that make their appearance in his stories are either prostitutes or unconvincing innocents ripe for rape and destruction. But for Traven this is a man's world. In fact, Traven's stories are not novels at all in the usual sense. They are more like tracts written in intense moral indignation. It is to their author's credit that they read with unflagging interest even without women and sex. Traven is continually the master storyteller reporting the horrible wickedness of the world. His ability to hold one spellbound while he recites these deeds is what establishes him as a great writer.

CHAPTER X

What was happening in the book trade, in other words, was about what was happening in the movies. But in the book trade, what was happening was more regretted. And for this reason—that the book trade prior to the twenties, had been an institution which prided itself upon accepting precisely the responsibilities its subsequent practice tended to evade. The book trade had been, indeed, one of the most responsible of all trades that men could practice. Books in the last century and the century before, were sold by men who knew them not as packages but as books—men who had, and were entitled to have, opinions about the content and the value of the books they sold ... men whose customers came to them, not to learn how many copies of a given novel had been sold before, but to talk about the novel itself, the innards of the novel—the quality of the book.

From "A Free Man's Books"
an address by ARCHIBALD MACLEISH
delivered at the annual banquet of the
American Booksellers Association, May 6, 1942

VARDIS FISHER

I n introducing my correspondence with Vardis Fisher I don't think I can improve on the introduction I wrote to my publication of his book of essays *The Neurotic Nightingale* in 1935. I reprint it here:

My customers and collector friends know that I am principally interested in young writers. By this I do not mean youthful in years, but authors who have issued only a few books and who are mostly unknown to the book-buying public. My reasons for this interest are twofold. In the first place these writers are usually the ones who have something to say; and in the second place, they need help. It is quite obvious that most of the best-selling authors of today do not need the bookseller's help. They have become a standard item like sugar in a grocery store.

Thus it happened that one day several years ago I ran across the name of Vardis Fisher. I wrote to his publisher, Houghton Mifflin, but they replied that his books were no longer published by them. I next wrote to the largest firm of wholesale booksellers in America, Baker & Taylor, and they likewise could give me no information about Fisher, nor could they immediately supply any of the author's books. It was several months before I discovered that a western firm by the name of the Caxton Printers, Ltd., in Caldwell, Idaho were the latest publishers of Vardis Fisher. Several days later I received and read *Dark Bridwell*, his second novel and third book.

It may be asked why I went to so much trouble about Fisher without, until then, having read any of his books. Because I had heard a rumor that Fisher could write and had something to say. It has been my habit to track down these rumors and, if I have been frequently disappointed, the occasions on which I found a gem have more than made up for it. I found a gem in Fisher.

Hurriedly I searched to find what else he had published and located two earlier books, *Sonnets to an Imaginary Madonna*, a slender volume of poetry issued in 1927, and *Toilers of the Hills*, a novel published in 1928. I learned at about the same time that a new book, to be called *In Tragic Life*, was coming out. I got the book and read it. I became so excited reading it that I placed the largest order I have ever given to a salesman for a novel by an unknown author. I sent it to a list of discriminating book collectors. Only one order was returned.

Here was originality and vigorous writing at its best. A simple story and yet one that held you gripped in a vise; a novel of adolescent suffering transformed into a tale of horror. This was achieved without any stylistic hocus-pocus. Fisher is a conventional writer. He has not invented a style as has Hemingway, in which, only too frequently, vacuity hides behind syntax; neither has he achieved any of the sleight of hand tricks of Faulkner. It is the cumulative effect of his careful observation, pitiless probing and devastating frankness, that leaves one prostrated.

The reviews of *In Tragic Life* were not as good as the book deserved, but they helped its sale. Slowly his books began to move and soon *Toilers of the Hills* went out of print. I am told the first editions of the other books will soon be exhausted. I felt happy that I was one of the first to draw attention to Fisher's books, but I would not be satisfied until I had published a book of his myself. It was not easy to accomplish this but because this preface is already longer than it ought to be, I will merely add: here is the book.

[After rereading the Schwartz–Fisher Correspondence it occurred to me that readers who had not lived through this period or read widely of this time in history might not understand the background against which these letters were written.

This was a time when writers, young and old, chose sides, either Left or Right. The writers for the Establishment were pretty well divided between the Right and the Left. Inevitably the younger writers were radical, and the older ones conservative. Also, the more significant writers, and that includes the poets and novelists, were heavily represented on the Left.

It was a time of ferment; of action; of movement. Here in America the John Reed Clubs were being formed; Writers' Congresses were being held; the Newspaper Guild was organized. In Europe the Nazis and the Fascisti were marching.

Even booksellers, who are generally nonpolitical, took sides. Neither of us were Communists, although we were both radical (in Fisher's words, "I am a pretty severe radical in all directions"), and it is in this spirit that the Fisher–Schwartz Correspondence should be read.]

DEAR MR. FISHER/DEAR MR. SCHWARTZ.
A CORRESPONDENCE*

(Several months ago the University of Idaho Library acquired manuscript copy of correspondence originated by Var-

---

* Reprinted by permission of the University of Idaho Library, March 18, 1975.

dis Fisher, native Idahoan and American man of letters (1895–1968), to Harry Schwartz, who was, and is, owner of the Schwartz Bookshop in Milwaukee, Wisconsin. The letters, which concern Fisher's work and his relations with publishers, were exchanged during the period November 1933 to May 1935. The Library does not possess manuscript copy of the letters initiated by Schwartz but was provided with xerox copy of these documents. Letters reprinted by kind permission of Mrs. Vardis Fisher and Mr. Harry Schwartz.)

November 21, 1933   Milwaukee, Wisconsin
Dear Mr. Fisher:

I wonder if you would write a preface to a forthcoming catalog of mine dealing exclusively with modern first editions.

My new series of catalogs will be prefaced by a collected author whose checklist the catalog will contain.

Although you have written comparatively few books yet, I have interested a large number of collectors in your first editions. Incidentally, it may interest you to know that I was one of the first booksellers to discover you and call your merit to the attention of people interested in contemporary American literature. Your publishers will acquaint you with my interest in you. Your foreword, should you wish to write it, will be in one sense unique as you are one of the very few authors who will appear in the series I intend to publish.

I suggested to your publishers that they increase the number of your limited editions as it is unquestionable that you are merely achieving a very small part of your sale today. Others will follow.

Will you please let me know at your earliest convenience about this foreword. This is the first time, I believe, that booksellers have tried to achieve contact with the author and it has been a great pleasure to recommend your books in particular to my collectors. By this time you will know exactly what I think of them. May you write many more.

Faithfully yours,
Harry Schwartz

November 28, 1933   University of Montana, Missoula
Dear Mr. Schwartz:

I have, it is true, heard from Mr. Gipson that you and some others have begun to look at me as a collectors' item. That is almost as flattering as it is terrifying. Perhaps, however, the flattery will wear the terror out.

I think I should be glad to try to do a preface for your catalog—but wonder if I can. Anyway, will you not give me a clear notion of what it is to be and what purpose you expect it to fulfill? I am a very ignorant person in such matters and your letter leaves me wholly in the dark.

Yours sincerely,
Vardis Fisher

December 1, 1933   Milwaukee, Wisconsin
Dear Mr. Fisher:

I have your most charming letter for which I thank you.

Yes, it is true that I am a discoverer of you. I had written to Baker & Taylor, the largest jobbers in America, but they had none of your books. I have since written them that they should stock them. When I found that Caxton bought your earlier books from Houghton & Vinal I wrote to ask how many they had on hand. I have already sold several hundred of your books and believe it is just a start. When I read *In Tragic Life*, a beautiful book, I immediately sat down and wrote to every collector to whom I had sold Faulkner. The response was splendid. Thirty-four orders came in the mail for this and earlier of your books. It so happened that I picked out Hemingway in 1925; Faulkner in 1926; Caldwell and you in 1931 and 1932. I am not so much a bookseller as an explorer in the realm of new writers. There are enough booksellers to handle the Hardys, Shaws, Barries and Stevensons; it is the unknown and unsung writers that I am particularly interested in. I was the first American bookman to catalog the works of Bates, Davies, Hanley and Manhood, all very young men and all very good writers. It seems that I am puffing myself along with the writers, something I don't want to do.

My catalogs are all out of print but I am sending you my own copies so that you can see what they are like. When you have finished with them you can return them to me, as I have no other copies for reference. I have tried to establish a long sought for intimacy between a rare book catalog and the collector. I have somewhat achieved this in my notes to the books cataloged. But I believe it would be a triumph to have each catalog prefaced by a young writer himself, in this way bringing the writer directly before the people who read his books, informally and not professionally.

In your article you can say what you please; it can be as long or as short as you wish. You can say something about book collecting if you want. One writer who is doing a preface for me is going to attack his publisher (who has just refused his last novel, calling it dirty). It would be very interesting, for instance, to know all about the publisher of your first book. Incidentally, I have completed a checklist of your books but can't find out how many copies were printed of *Sonnets to an*

Imaginary Madonna. I wrote to Vinal but he has not answered. Gipson doesn't know. Would you mind telling me?

This letter seems terribly long and I hope you will forgive me. Perhaps you know what I want.

Faithfully yours,
Harry Schwartz

December 14, 1933   Ririe, Idaho
Dear Mr. Schwartz:

Herewith is my attempt at a short introduction for one of your catalogs.

I deliberated book collecting but know so little about it that I felt inadequate there; and there is really nothing to make a preface of in the materials relating to the publication of my first book. If what I send is not what you want, do not hesitate to throw it away.

I don't know how many copies of *Sonnets* Vinal published. My relations with Vinal were most unhappy—indeed, most unfortunate; and what he did or did not do I've never been able to learn. He violated his contract with me and the matter of the *Sonnets* is still hanging fire.

And many thanks for your interest in my work.

Yours sincerely,
Vardis Fisher

December 22, 1933   Milwaukee, Wisconsin
Dear Mr. Fisher:

I am in receipt of your magnificent preface, for which I do not know how to thank you enough. Instead of holding this over for a later catalog I am going to issue it in my first number, together with a checklist of your works. I wonder if you have any material published that I should know about that I may be able to include this in my checklist of your books.

As you know, I have made several excursions into the publishing field and it would be a great pleasure for me to publish something of yours. Perhaps you have a short story or two that I can issue in a limited signed edition. Of course I would pay you the regular rates. Publishing with me is more a sport than it is a business. When I find someone whom I like tremendously, as I like you, I want to publish a book of his.

I am sending you a copy of my publication *Salmagundi* by William Faulkner. I will also send you my little book on *This Book Collecting Racket* when it is ready that you may see some of the pitfalls you must try to avoid. A copy of the catalog will go off to you immediately as it is ready.

With best wishes,
Harry Schwartz

December 27, 1933   Milwaukee, Wisconsin
Dear Mr. Fisher:

I have completed my checklist of your works and I wonder if you would object to me using part of your letter regarding Vinal and the *Sonnets*. This is the part I would like to use: "I don't know how many copies of *Sonnets* Vinal published. My relations with Vinal were most unhappy—indeed, most unfortunate; and what he did or did not do I've never been able to learn. He violated his contract with me and the matter of the *Sonnets* is still hanging fire."

My reason for desiring to use this is two-fold. I would like to have it known how Vinal treated you and, secondly, it would be a good thing to expose this cheat so as to keep him from cheating others. Of course if you have any objection I will not use it. Would you mind letting me know at once as the catalog is going to the printers in a day or so.

Faithfully yours,
Harry Schwartz

December 28, 1933   Ririe, Idaho
Dear Mr. Schwartz:

I am glad you like the preface. I look forward eagerly to *This Book Collecting Racket* and I'll be watching for the pitfalls. I tumble into plenty of them.

Besides my five books (including the one to appear Jan. 3) and a little fugitive verse, I have published only:

> *In Defense of Profanity*, Brentano's BookChat, March–April 1929
>
> *Myths About Authors*, The Frontier, March 1933
>
> *The Mother*, Frontier and Midland, November 1933

The Mother is my only published short story. It stirred up some good comment and is to be reprinted by Uzzell; and O'Brien, who wrote me from England, is going to give it some stars (******) or whatever, in his strange way, he accords in grading stories as if they were potatoes.

I hardly have anything which you could publish now for the fun of it; but I intend to get a couple of stories out within the coming year and possibly later I might have something that you would regard as worth the bother.

And many thanks.

Yours sincerely,
Vardis Fisher

January 4, 1934   Ririe, Idaho
Dear Mr. Schwartz:

I'd rather you would not quote me in your catalog in regard to the Vinal matter. My opinion of him, it is true, would demand strong language. But he is now out of the publishing business; and he was only one, after all, of a group of shyster publishers who preyed on authors who had more vanity than sense. That, in part, was my trouble in 1927, and I dare say the experience serves me right.

The Caxton Printers are now buying the rights and remaining stock from Humphries; and after all these years, I may get a penny of royalty. The really humorous thing about it all, I think, is the fact that a man so unconscionable in his dealings should be among our principal editors of poetry magazines.

Yours sincerely,
Vardis Fisher

I am so far from a post office that this letter may be delayed. I'm sorry.

January 8, 1934   Milwaukee, Wisconsin
Dear Mr. Fisher:

I rushed out to the library and read *The Mother*, which I think is one of the finest short stories I have ever read. I am awfully sorry that it is coming out in book form as I would break my neck to publish it otherwise.

Are you not mistaken about *Myths About Authors* appearing in the Frontier of March 1933? At this time the Frontier had suspended publication and it was not until November that it merged with the Midland. Sadly enough, neither of these magazines is listed in the periodical index so I cannot locate your article. Possibly it appeared some other place. Would you mind telling me if it did?

Your telling me that you may have something to publish later in the year gives me hope. I hate to pester you and so will not mention this again until you have something that I can publish. I would like, if possible, to include the Bookchat article and the *Myths About Authors* if you would let me reprint them.

I have just finished *Passions Spin the Plot* and am still excited. Have you finished volume three yet?

I note what you say about Vinal and I will remove this from the catalog. I understand your attitude perfectly. It is, however, a shame that this fellow cannot be exposed.

Sincerely,
Harry Schwartz

September 4, 1934   Ririe, Idaho

Dear Mr. Schwartz:

From one of your customers who implores my signature there comes your checklist of my stuff carrying my preface which I did for you last fall. Is it possible for you to send me a few copies of this? And I have recently seen some reviews of *This Book Collecting Racket*, a copy of which you promised me, and to which I am looking forward with much interest.

I think I did not thank you for the copy of *Salmagundi*.

You may be interested to know that Doubleday, Doran and I have been having a merry time over my third volume in the tetralogy. The movie censorship business has them scared and in consequence I've had to make a few minor concessions to the pure; but I don't believe I let any blood. If they do not back out again the volume will appear about January 4.

I wonder if it is not your opinion that the Caxton Printers are publishing too many copies of the first editions of my stuff. 2,000 seem to be unnecessary. Gipson, of course, under present arrangements must confine his trade to those who want a first edition copy and to dealers in first editions; and it seems to me that so large an edition as he puts out defeats itself.

I still remember your wish to publish something of mine. Would you be interested in three or four essays which the "literary" magazines have seen and have declared to be heresy?

Sincerely,

Vardis Fisher

September 9, 1934   Milwaukee, Wisconsin

Dear Mr. Fisher:

I am in receipt of your letter and regret that you did not receive the checklist I mailed to you last summer. Under separate cover I am sending you several copies.

You write that you did not receive any copies of *This Book Collecting Racket* either, although I inscribed part two and mailed it off to you last June. Possibly this was misdirected and, as I would like to have you see both of these parts, I am inscribing two more copies to you at once. I regret that part one is out of print but if you would like to have a few extra copies of part two do not hesitate to tell me and I will send them.

The news about your third book does not surprise me. Doran together with other publishers are becoming extremely cautious. Would 10 percent royalties on the list price be satisfactory? Incidentally, did you finish the essays? If you did I would like to get busy on the book immediately, as I am having difficulty with Dutton's, who control the rights of Crowley's book *The Diary of a Drug Fiend*.

The business came in from Guggenheim. I reported what I thought of you and your work and sent Mr. Moe, secretary, my pamphlets, marking for him the paragraphs of your work. Since then he has thanked me for having sent them.

Let me know what you think of all the above and I remain as ever

Faithfully yours,

Harry Schwartz

October 16, 1934   Milwaukee, Wisconsin
Dear Mr. Fisher:

I am planning to bring out an edition of Crowley's *Diary of a Drug Fiend* very shortly, but as I have already announced your book of essays for publication in my catalog, I would prefer to issue your volume first.

Perhaps you were too busy to answer my last letter to you and so I am writing you again for the essays. Please let me know by return.

With best personal regards, I am

Faithfully yours,
Harry Schwartz

October 25, 1934   Ririe, Idaho
Dear Mr. Schwartz:

The checklists and your two monographs came some time ago and the latter I read and read again. They are excellent and depressing. They are depressing because I was flabbergasted to learn that such writers as Robert Nathan are still, or were until recently, remaindered— Faulkner, too. You could have knocked my eyes off. *This Book Collecting Racket* is now traveling and is somewhere near Boise. A lot of persons are reading it and ten to one I'll never get it back.

The essays I spoke of you may have to wait quite a while for. The truth is that I read them after a month or two and feel that I must again revise them; and read and revise again. This process I pursue with morbid endlessness.

I am asking for a Guggenheim fellowship and am giving your name as a reference. I hope you don't mind. I see no reason why a dealer in firsts should not be among the references. I think, in fact, he should be. The materials from the Secretary will reach you in short time. This is my third request for a fellowship on that foundation. It will be my last.

Sincerely,
Vardis Fisher

October 26, 1934   Ririe, Idaho
Dear Mr. Schwartz:

I wish to apologize for my long delay in answering your letter. I went down to Ririe today to register my application to the Guggenheim Foundation, taking with me a letter to you; and I received yours of October 16. In the first place, I get my mail irregularly and infrequently because I have to go eighteen miles for it. In the second place, I have been, as I declared in my letter of yesterday, working over these essays without yet getting them as I want them.

Do write and tell me how soon you must have these. I've written my publishers to learn if they approve; and I'll get busy on the essays at once, though to do so I have to lay aside a novel. Meanwhile, remembering that you also wanted to include a short story, I suggest you might have a look at the one in October 15 *Direction*, the quarterly just out. I don't want you to include any story that you do not believe to be worthy.

Could you publish Crowley first and so give me a little more time? I don't like to let these things out of my hands until they're as good as I can make them.

Sincerely,
Vardis Fisher

.

December 1, 1934   The Caxton Printers, Caldwell, Idaho
Dear Mr. Schwartz:

A few days ago I came to Caldwell and have talked with Mr. Gipson about the matter of your bringing out something of mine and he wrote to Mr. Maule of Doubleday, Doran and Company. Maule writes:

> I agree with you that so long as Fisher does nothing that would class as a full length book for Casanova, it is all right for him to do a small paper-bound pamphlet to be distributed among collectors.

This restriction, together with another—reserving the right to reprint whatever you publish in a book of essays later—may be too severe. But there is nothing I can do about it. When an author is tied up he is tied up.

Please let me know what you think. I am awfully sorry that I have no power to allow you to go ahead and do what you had in mind to do. I never imagined my publishers would crack down on me in this.

Sincerely,
Vardis Fisher

December 7, 1934   Milwaukee, Wisconsin
Dear Mr. Fisher:

I am in receipt of your letter and am distressed at the information you send me. But my desire to publish something of yours is so great that even though it is a small book I will still like to do it.

How long are the essays you have? Do you think that Doran would object to a small book bound either in boards or stiff paper covers enclosed in a slipcase similar to *Salmagundi* if it did not run over 100 pages. What does Mr. Gipson think about this? This would still make a fairly presentable book and, although it would be slim in appearance, it would, of course, be a collectors' item.

Yes, I believe the 2,000 copies of the Caxton first edition are too many. It seems that 1,000 would be enough to an intelligent limitation. They must remember that Doran will get the trade orders for the book; their salesmen cover the country and visit most of the little and big shops. Caxton will get the rare book trade orders but they are comparatively few. They should realize that whenever I will sell 50 copies of your book, a firm like Edgar Wells who does one hundred times more business than I do won't sell any. Wells is not interested in living authors, but sticks to Shaw, Wells, Hardy, Moore, etc. It's the young blood in the rare book business that is responsible for Hemingway, Faulkner, Caldwell, Bates, Davies, Manhood and yourself. The Rosenbachs, Drakes and Wells haven't even heard of you.

But enough of this, here in my pamphlets I go into them in detail.

Send me your essays at once. Nothing would give me greater pleasure than to publish them. The more heretical the better. Would you include the story "The Scarecrow" with them or probably you have another story.

A story or two would give the book the needed touch to be an item.

Let me know what you think of the "Racket" and send on the essays.

Faithfully yours,
Harry Schwartz

December 14, 1934   Milwaukee, Wisconsin
Dear Mr. Fisher:

I do not know whether or not you would wish to have a preface to the book of yours I plan to publish. Perhaps you would not; if so do not hesitate to tell me. On the other hand you would unquestionably like to see what I have written for it. If you think it is proper please tell me.

How is your novel coming along? I am out getting as many orders for it as I can.

With kindest regards and best wishes, I remain

Faithfully yours,
Harry Schwartz

December 15, 1934   The Caxton Printers, Caldwell, Idaho
Dear Mr. Schwartz:

I don't have enough essays to run to a hundred pages. I have, in fact, only two, which would run to about thirty-five or forty. I think to include a story with these two essays (which are of a piece) would not be good. These two would make an item. They are two of the best I shall ever do.

The terms as you suggested in your last letter are all right but I do hope you can run me off about 25 copies to give to my friends. These need not be numbered, and, of course, need not be signed.

Mr. Gipson declares that the contract must contain the following provisos:

1. That your distribution shall be confined to collectors.

2. That you must give other dealers a chance at whatever number of copies they wish to order in advance. He means, of course, dealers in firsts like yourself who are interested in my stuff; and insists he cannot afford to alienate their goodwill by denying to them a Fisher item in which they may be interested. He adds, further, that you should allow them the customary discount on the trade list. Such dealers' names he would furnish you and he proposes that you approach them yourself for advance orders. I have no notion whether this proviso will displease you.

3. That your copyright will cover only this special printing so that Caxton and Doubleday can include these two essays in a book of essays which I have in mind for publication three or four years hence.

4. That you may, under these restrictions, issue the item in paper, boards, or cloth as you please.

Let me know if these provisos allow you to go ahead. If so, I shall send the essays at once. They are ready.

Sincerely,
Vardis Fisher

December 19, 1934   Milwaukee, Wisconsin

Dear Mr. Fisher:

I have your letter and note that you have only two essays which would run to about thirty-five or forty pages. I am afraid this would not be enough and I would like to include the short story from *Direction*. Even this would make it a tiny volume but it might be stretched out to fifty or sixty pages and I think I can make it attractive.

In your letter of September fourth you said you had three or four essays. Perhaps you have decided that only two are of importance.

Would you mind my quoting in a prospectus from your letter of September fourth the plain fact that three or four of these essays were seen by the "literary" magazines and were declared to be heresy? I have no objections to any of the provisos of Mr. Gipson. To the contrary, the four points are precisely what I have always carried out as a principle. I have always given dealers in first editions the privilege of ordering as many copies in advance as they wanted. Frequently this has taken copies away from my own sale but I prefer not to let my publishing activity interfere with my bookselling. Gipson may send me a list of dealers to whom I will send prospectuses. I will be glad to send you twenty-five copies which will be an out of series specially prepared for you for presentation purposes. These will not be numbered. You can, however, sign them if you wish. I prefer not to number them as dealers become indignant and rightfully over a larger issue than is advertised and in my issuing of books I try to be as fair to other dealers as I would like publishers to be fair to me as a bookseller.

I believe this includes everything. About the story I can take it from *Direction* unless you care to make any changes for its publication in a book. Let me know about this and send off the essays at once.

Faithfully yours,
Harry Schwartz

December 22, 1934   Caldwell, Idaho
Dear Mr. Schwartz:

I am leaving Caldwell for Ririe in the morning; and inasmuch as I did not want to take the essays along with me I sent them off to you this morning, together with your introduction; and just now have your letter of the nineteenth.

Your introduction first: this, I feel, is a matter to be left to you. I see no reason why your little volume should not have a preface if you wish to give it one.

In regard to the *Direction* story: I strongly feel that it would look rather silly in a volume with the two essays I have sent, and, after reading the essays, I think you'll feel the same way. It is true that I did have, in fact, four essays and they are in a way all of a piece, but not a piece as the two are that I sent. Both, moreover, stand in need of much revision; and for one I have a bit of distaste, not knowing whether it really says what

I wanted to say. Just the same I shall, if you can give me the time, try my level best to work one of them out for you; do this during the holidays; and get it off to you by about the first of the year.

In regard to quoting in your prospectus from my letter: the editors (bless them) did not call the essays heresy but I inferred from the agent's letter that they did object to them on some such ground. After you read the essays you will know pretty certainly why the editors did not want them. After I return to Ririe I'll look the agent's letter up and see if there is not something in it by way of statement that you can use. But how could the damned "literary" editors be interested in my stuff? In the last Scribner's (and Scribner's is about the best of the five) there is an article declaring that the world of science has returned to God. It is one of the feeblest evasions I've ever seen; and if that's the sort of stuff Scribner's subscribers want, then my essays are heretical and with a vengeance.

I'll tell Gipson you find the provisos acceptable. Everything now is, I think, clear between us. I'll do my damndest on that essay; and if it's a bit late reaching you it will be because I'm snowbound. It's a ten-mile trip on skis, you know, after my mail—once a week.

The season's greetings, and may your martinis be good.

Sincerely,
Vardis Fisher

December 29, 1934 Milwaukee, Wisconsin
Dear Mr. Fisher:

I received your letter and carefully noted what you have to say about the story. As you feel this way about it I will not include it with the essays but I will wait for the third essay you are working on now. Please send it to me as quickly as it is ready.

If you find anything for me to quote, fine, otherwise I'll do my best with what I have.

With best wishes and hoping you get a break with *We Are Betrayed* I am

Faithfully yours,
Harry Schwartz

December 31, 1934   Ririe, Idaho

Dear Mr. Schwartz:

Herewith are two essays instead of one to complete your item. It will not be necessary now to use the story, which would be absurdly out of place. Herewith, too, is a prefatory note which I should like to have included.

> Of these, except the first, which I've never offered, Curtis Brown wrote: "In Defense of Professors" is the best addition to Educatiana that we have ever seen.... We have enjoyed "How's Your Sense of Humor" and "Some Implications of Radicalism" tremendously. We are determined that Harper's will take you up to carry on with whatever you are going to write... .

The letter returning the articles I cannot find but I recall that it declared all the editors praised the writing but shied from the material. "Professors" was returned separately and I have a copy of the Harper's letter rejecting it. It says: "This is a good piece but somehow we are a bit cool to it. It is hard to say quite why: it may be a feeling that the author wobbles between cynicism and idealism and gives an odd effect." But that, of course, was an evasion.

In your prospectus I think you might say if you wish:

> Three of the four essays were rejected by all the "quality" magazines. The editors praised the writing but for reasons that

should be clear to anyone they seemed to be afraid of the material. What Fisher has to say in these essays is not the sort of thing that most people like to have said.

I send, too, a list of persons to whom I hope you will send a copy of the prospectus, including myself; and I hope you will later furnish me the names of those who did not buy for to some of them I shall wish to send an unnumbered copy. If Gipson hasn't sent a list of other dealers I suggest you write him for it.

Here's wishing you much luck in this publishing venture and a corking good 1935.

Sincerely,
Vardis Fisher

January 8, 1935   Milwaukee, Wisconsin
Dear Mr. Fisher:

I received the essays with the prefatory note and your letter. I would like to make some remarks about the essays but am so very busy that I will reserve them for a later letter.

I will use what you have in the prospectus, which I am working on now. I have as yet not obtained an estimate from my printer so am still uncertain as to the price. I would like to publish not more than 500 copies. I will, of course, send prospectuses to the people you mention, including yourself.

Mr. Gipson has not sent me a list that he wants me to circularize but I wrote him I would be glad to send him as many prospectuses as he needs.

I note that you plan to place some of your copies with critics. I did not know that you wanted to do this because I had already planned to send out a dozen copies for review. As it would be pointless to send two copies to the same person for review I am enclosing a list of people I plan to send review copies. Perhaps you would prefer to send these copies out for review yourself. If you have reasons for doing so kindly advise me and I won't send out review copies at all.

Harry Schwartz

January 19, 1935   Ririe, Idaho

Dear Mr. Schwartz:

I infer from your letters that you do not care for the essays. Do not publish these if they don't hit you right.

I've written Doubleday Doran to ask if they have any objection to your sending out a few copies to critics. If these are sent it will be best for you to send them. Of your list, Brickell, Soskin, and Benet are three to whom I'd never myself send copies. These men can't see me at all.... And I feel a copy ought to go to certain critics who have been unusually understanding of my work or who I am sure would not wish to be left out. Chief of these are Jordan-Smith of *Los Angeles Times*, Webster Jones of *Portland Oregonian*, Howard Wolf of *Akron Beacon-Journal*, Laruis Lindemann of Denver, and Louis Zucker of the University of Utah, Salt Lake, who reviews for the *Deseret News*.

Tell me frankly what you feel about the essays. I know there are questions in your mind. I know you are interested in my work and shall be glad always to have your most candid opinions.

Sincerely,
Vardis Fisher

January 26, 1935   Milwaukee, Wisconsin

Dear Mr. Fisher:

I am sorry I could not answer your letter earlier but I have been kept busy. Will soon write you a long letter about the essays.

I agree with you about Brickell, Soskin and Benet. When Benet reviewed *Passions* I became so furious that I wrote him what I thought of him. The other two are just lackeys working for the capitalist press. Yet they have a large public and it is important to get the book noticed. But if you would rather I didn't send them copies I won't. To hell with them. I am making a note of the others you want copies sent to and will see to it that they get them.

Faithfully yours,
Harry Schwartz

February 22, 1935   Milwaukee, Wisconsin
Dear Mr. Fisher:

This is the first breathing spell I have had so here goes for a long letter. My feelings about the essays are strange. Of course I am going to publish them; in fact, they are in the press right now and under separate cover I am sending you a prospectus. But because I want you to understand how I feel about them I will go into it a little.

I might explain that there are several reasons to publish a collected author in a limited edition. Most regular publishers issue a limited edition because they make money on it. It does not cost a cent more for the printing as they use the same plates for both editions—that they also publish a trade edition. The only other reason for the publishing of a limited edition is for fun, or glory, or for the sake of literature or whatever you want to call it. In this case it is unlikely that any money will be made. Now I like your work a hell of a lot. I've shouted your praises to everybody that comes into my store. To my mail order customers whom I cannot reach by voice, I have written letters and sent catalogs and announcements. I have even written to other dealers calling their attention to you. I have done so much yelling about Fisher that dealers have sent me orders for your books thinking that I must be your publisher.

I thought of your work so highly that nothing in the world would give me more pleasure than to publish a book of yours myself. I knew I could make no money on it; in fact, I knew that I would lose money on it as I lost money on Faulkner's book. I had a volume of Bates' stories that he wanted me to publish for almost a year, wondering if I could afford to publish them. I would have to lose about five hundred dollars on the job and finally returned them to him. Rhys Davies asked if I wanted to publish a novel of his that nobody in England or America would tackle. (By the way, I almost went to jail for importing Davies' first novel, *The Withered Root,* and defended it in court, winning a decision for the book.) I wanted to but my printer advised me against it. It could cost me one thousand dollars. Hanley had a novel something like his *German Prisoner* for importing of which I almost again went to jail, and he wanted me to publish it. It would cost me seven hundred and fifty dollars and possibly a jail sentence, certainly a fine. But even though I would lose money on your book the thought of publishing you kept me awake nights.

I looked forward to your work with great pleasure. When the essays came I was disappointed. I read them carefully but wondered! Probably I was expecting too much or probably I am a dumb bastard; but I did not think them of great consequence. Of course, they would make a book and I would sell copies to collectors. I did not think I could shout about them to the world or offer to fight anyone who spoke disparagingly about them as I would do with your novels and short stories. The book would make an item, but my heart was not in them. I do not have the essays here so it is difficult to make the points I would like to. Like the articles in the *Nation* and *New Republic* they do not get anywhere.

Frankly, the first essay was a puzzle to me. After reading it several times I felt bewildered. The satire, if it was meant for satire, escaped me.

The second baffled me also but your attack on Communism seems to be out of place. That Russia has transferred the symbols of power from wealth to office is no reason to attack Communism. You seem to think the dictatorship of the proletariat and capitalist dictatorship are the same. But as Bukharin says—"the formal side of the matter alone ('dictatorship' in general), does not decide anything: the important thing is its class meaning; its content—material and ideological; the dynamics of its development; its relationship to the general current of world historical development. The dictatorship of the proletariat and the dictatorship of the capitalists are polar opposites, and their content and historical significance are entirely different."

You may despise me for saying some of these things but you are the last man in the world I want to be dishonest with.

Faithfully yours,
Harry Schwartz

P.S. Let me know what you think of the prospectus.

March 4, 1935   Ririe, Idaho

Dear Mr. Schwartz:

Nothing in the past few years of my life has so distressed me as the fact that you have gone ahead with the essays, feeling as you do. It is absurd to say, as you do, that I may despise you for some of the statements in your letter of February 22. I should have been pained if you had not been frank; and frankness impels me to say that you merit a thorough-going rebuke for going ahead with stuff when your heart is not in it.

I can, I think, understand your point of view as a publisher: if I had money, I should take profound pleasure in publishing something now and then which I like and thought deserving but which commercial publishers would not understand. But I understand, too, that the experience would be tasteless and pointless if I did not feel enthusiasm for what I undertook. And there was no reason for your going ahead: if you had sent the essays back, saying they had disappointed you, I'd not have been offended at all; and I feel so deeply about the matter now that I urge you, if the matter has not gone too far, to cancel the project and I'll try to pay what the prospectus and preliminary work has cost you. I don't want anything of mine published by anyone who does not want to publish it.

I surmised weeks ago that you were disappointed but I had no idea you'd go ahead before writing me. In trying to understand the source of your disappointment, I came to the conclusion that you must be a Marxist. Now I am not a Marxist for reasons which I shall try to make clear in my fourth volume; but some of my closest friends are and I have much in common with their political thesis. Do not fancy, on the other hand, that I am a Nazi, or that I am not a pretty severe radical in all directions.

It would be in bad taste to try to persuade you to like essays which you do not like. I shall attempt nothing of that sort. But I do wish to say that these four are by implication, in my opinion, a pretty devastating assault on all the orthodox ideologies and that the second especially lands right in the guts of the Nazi stronghold. But why go on? I feel sick about the matter and if there's any getting out of it at this stage, please do. There are so many things that ought to be published which would enlist your sympathies and whether these of mine are published now really doesn't matter to me at all.

Let me know at once what if anything we can do.

Sincerely,

Vardis Fisher

If you feel, by the way, that the Chamberlains and Benets and Soskins will give a favorable review of these, then your guess is certainly not mine.

March 12, 1935   Milwaukee, Wisconsin

Dear Mr. Fisher:

It is difficult to reply to your letter without giving way to emotion. Had I known that you would feel so strongly I would not have written you about the essays at all. They are in the press now and I expect to work on the proofs in a day or so. I have taken eighteen advance orders from collectors and fifty-three advance orders from dealers. It would be most embarrassing to cancel the project now. Moreover, I still want to publish them. I think so highly of your work that the publishing of the essays has become a labor of love, even though I think they are not your best work. Remember also that I am a fellow given to great enthusiasms and equally great dejections. Your work has fascinated me, that is the important thing.

I don't think we are really opposed to each other on fundamentals. I am going through a transition politically and resented one or two of your statements. Had I thought less of you, I should have ignored them; but what you say has become to me more a personal matter than a critical one.

What you say about Benet *et al.* is correct. I believed it necessary to get the book noticed, even if the reviews were unfavorable, but there will be enough places to put copies so that we can ignore them. I'll try to get your copies to you as early as possible. In about a week I will have my printer send you the limitation sheet for your signature. If you will get these off quickly the binder will be able to start immediately.

Faithfully yours,
Harry Schwartz

P.S. I'd like to send you an article on "Capitalism and Book Collecting" if you are not too busy to look at it.

March 17, 1935   Ririe, Idaho
Dear Mr. Schwartz:

It does seem impossible to retreat now, and I can only grin about it and be damned sorry that you went ahead. I shall wish to see the galley proof and can get it back to you within the week of its coming. I shall make very few changes but I do want to have a final look; and if you will indicate by query in the galley the statements that left you most dubious, I'll give them prolonged thought.

The matter of critics I leave entirely to you. As I said, I don't expect favorable reviews from most of the good fascists: I may not be a Marxist but fascists find me more intolerable than Mike Gold.

I hope you get your money out of this venture.

Sincerely,
Vardis Fisher

March 22, 1935   Milwaukee, Wisconsin
Dear Mr. Fisher:

I just received your letter and am terribly sorry that the galleys were sent to my printer in Manitowoc several days ago. I am afraid he had already run the book off but I am writing him immediately. Had you told me earlier that you wanted to see the galleys I would have mailed them direct to you but I believed you went through the essays carefully and wanted them to stand as written. I really do not feel that you should have made any revisions to please me.

By this time you should have the limitation sheets for your signature. Please return these to the printer as quickly as possible.

Faithfully yours,
Harry Schwartz

April 12, 1935   Ririe, Idaho
Dear Mr. Schwartz:

The limitation sheets for the signatures have not come. I hope they have not miscarried.

Sincerely,
Vardis Fisher

April 15, 1935   Milwaukee, Wisconsin
Dear Mr. Fisher:

Thank you for your note that you have not received the limitation page for your signature. I am writing to my printer to find out what has happened. I have a long letter I want to write to you but will have to delay it for several days.

One of my customers whom I have recently interested in your work writes if he can obtain a picture of you. He says he does not want to ask you for them as he "might make you feel like a Hollywood actor dealing with one of his fans." I don't know whether you have any pictures of yourself or not but if you do, and if you don't mind, will you send me two.

With best wishes, I remain

Faithfully yours,
Harry Schwartz

April 28, 1935   Ririe, Idaho
Dear Mr. Schwartz:

   I received the limitation sheets today and shall get them off
at once.... I haven't a single photograph of myself. The only
good ones I've had done in the last two years were by the
Melander Studio, Higgins Avenue, Missoula, Montana. The
photographer said he would keep the plates and send out
copies at 25¢ each or you can write to Gipson for a copy, or
perhaps Maule of Doubleday, Doran has an extra.

   On an income of $700 a year I simply can't afford to have
any more made up.

   I'm interested in that long letter you promise and hope it
shows up. I hope, too, you have no trouble in moving the
printing. In the matter of critics do as you please, but I hope
you don't overlook Lovett of the *New Republic*. As for the
fascist boys in high places, I don't care: it's all up to you.

                                           Sincerely,
                                           Vardis Fisher

May 1, 1935   Milwaukee, Wisconsin
Dear Mr. Fisher:

   I received your letter today and am surprised that you just
received the signature sheets. My printer has double-crossed
me again, I suppose, because he wrote me that they were sent
to you more than two weeks ago. Orders have been pretty fair,
although a good many dealers upon whom I depended have
not ordered a single copy. The Argus Shop, the largest in
Chicago, has not ordered any; Drake, the largest in N.Y.,
ordered one copy, etc.

   I have pondered your essays considerably and because I
believed I might be mistaken in my conclusions, I read "Some
Implications of Radicalism" before the local John Reed Club.
I did not expect the attack that followed and, oddly enough,

found myself defending you. I don't understand how you of all people fail to see that the Communist way is the only solution to our troubles. Not to support the party, which needs every ally to keep us from fascism, is grievous enough, but to attack it besides is dangerous. I am convinced that we will either find ourselves in concentration camps (they are building several in California today) or in the Communist Party. You write that you would like to see a new party. This is really lending support to the Coughlins and Longs. They would very much like to see a new party. They would very much like to see the C.P. split up, and Christ knows it is split up enough already. Whatever your grievances are against the C.P., and from your essay I was unable to determine just what they were, you must realize that it is our only solution. Surely you cannot believe that we plot wars because of a "periodic need to express ourselves in vigorous action and to fulfill our racial memory and our heritage." These are the reasons that Hearst gives the people in his poisonous papers. A careful reading of modern history will show that all wars have their origin in economics. The contests, of course, were not always confined to the economic field but spread to every aspect of human consciousness.

Again I do not agree with you that "we use wars and hatred as instruments of regeneration and social changes are paid off in violence and murder." And when you say that Communists frankly declare this to be so it is not true. Communists are as keen as the most extreme pacifist on minimizing the degree of violence which will occur and which is now occurring in the world. We do know, however, that Capitalism will fight to the death in an attempt to maintain its privileges. It is only necessary to look about us today to see that this is true.

Who calls in the thugs to beat up the workers and who are the first to start violence on picket lines? Who was responsible for the terror in San Francisco, Toledo and Minneapolis? In our own state in Racine we have had a reign of terror for almost a year instituted and supported by the Racine Chamber of Commerce and the American Legion.

If you imply that murder and violence and hatred are "cunningly disguised aphrodisiacs" of Communism, I disagree with you. It would be impossible for you to prove these charges and I believe they are false. And I am unable to understand the considerable part of your essay dealing with sexual starvation, shame and guilt, hairless savages and dark impetuous emotions. If you mean that Communists are sexually starved, hairless savages with feelings of guilt and shame, I can only answer that it is not true.

I have no interest in defending the Socialists or Progressives and your statement that they all quarrel among themselves is quite true. So do thieves quarrel when they split up their booty or when one of them cheats another. The quarrels, however, of Communists are not caused by the reasons you enumerate. Lenin did not quarrel with Kautsky because he wished to glorify himself; not because he was the most egocentric; not because he was the most in danger of excesses of paranoia. Nor did Stalin quarrel with Trotsky because of an overwhelming self-love or mighty ambition denied. To believe that these are the reasons for the quarrels of these men is to misunderstand them sadly. I do not believe that you understand the depths of the class struggle, if you interpret those historic words as meaning human beings are your enemies. Your last two paragraphs strike me as being obscure and mystical. What you mean by a "thorough and uncompromising realism of the kind that Marxists have apparently never dreamed of"—I don't know.

Your letter made me horribly despondent. To know that you have to live on seven hundred dollars a year while the sons of bitches not worth a hair on their heads suck the teats of Mammon complacently, makes me want to cut my throat. But we still have the Revolution and, in the words of our forefathers, I greet you in its name.

Faithfully yours,
Harry Schwartz

May 11, 1935   Milwaukee, Wisconsin
Dear Mr. Fisher:

I called for one hundred copies of the book day before yesterday and sent out some to the most impatient collectors who had ordered. I expect the balance to be delivered in a day or so. Will send you copies as quickly as they come in.

If you do not mind I would like to use a few of your twenty-five copies for review purposes, because I am afraid there will not be enough perfect copies to go around. It appears that there was a shortage on the first signature, and although I will have copies without the first signature, there will barely be three-hundred good copies that I may number. If you object, however, to my using any of the twenty-five copies I will take them from the numbered and signed copies.

I am sending review copies to the following people: Paul Jordan-Smith, Webster Jones, Howard Wolfe, L. Lindemann, Louis Sucker, Robert M. Lovett, H. W. Wilson, Harry Hansen, *American Bookcollector Weekly*. If there are any others to whom you want review copies sent let me know. Also give me the address of the *Portland Oregonian*, the *Akron Beacon-Journal* and the address of L. Lindemann in Denver.

The following people did not buy or order the book from your list sent to me. You asked me to notify you; Myrtle Austin, B. Roland Lewis, Louis Zucker, L. A. Quivey, George

Thomas, Esther Nelson, F. W. Reynolds, Rev. Jacob Trapp, Betty Blair, Eva Hollis, H. G. Merriam, Andrew Corry, Philip O. Keeney, Barney Hewitt, Edmund Freeman, H. A. Watt, V. E. Fisher, Hal White, Dr. Clamor Gavin, R. I. Jones, James T. Chord, Richard Lake, Nona Tatum Siegler, Mrs. George Buhn, Grace Stone Coates, P. Hopkins, Robert B. Sweet, Jerome Cruskin.

Faithfully yours,
Harry Schwartz

May 15, 1935   Milwaukee, Wisconsin

Dear Mr. Fisher

Under separate cover I have forwarded twenty-five copies of *The Neurotic Nightingale* for yourself. I also have forwarded two numbered copies in accordance with your order. You will note that I did not take any copies of the twenty-five I promised you for presentation. These are also signed copies as it appears you signed a few more copies than the 300 which the edition was limited to for sale. Mr. Maresch believed it was wise to protect himself by doing this in case there would be any damaged copies which would not be able to be bound. There were about five bad copies which will not be sold. I preferred to send you the signed copies, as you will presumably wish to present them rather than send you a number of copies printed but unsigned and unnumbered for review. These I have sent out to the list submitted to you several days ago. If there are any friends or reviewers or critics to whom you would like to have me send a few unsigned and unnumbered copies please let me know. I have a few that I can put at your disposal.

I am sending a photograph of you that I bought from Mr. Gipson. Would you do me the favor to sign this for me that I may frame it for my personal collection? I'm also sending you three copies of the book, one for myself, one for my secretary, Fannie Shoor, and one for my very good friend, Don Smith. Would you mind inscribing these copies to us respectively? Number one is for Smith, number two for me and number three for Shoor.

Faithfully yours,
Harry Schwartz

May 30, 1935   Ririe, Idaho

Dear Mr. Schwartz:

The twenty-five copies came but not the three numbered ones which you said you were sending.... I am leaving within the week for Iowa City, where I shall be with a friend until August 1. You can address me care of Don Lewis, E 119 East Hall, Univ. of Iowa.... I like the appearance of the Essays, though there are two or three bad typographical errors.... Your long letter about the Marxist position I am answering for the moment by sending to you a part of what will be a chapter in the fourth volume of my tetralogy.

I wish you to consider this most carefully and to answer the arguments if you can. The last Marxist who attempted to answer did nothing but to fly into a self-pitying crusade and to end up by saying, "I don't know my reasons for being a Marxist and I don't give a damn." He said, "I'd not mind at all lining up a few of the middle-class and potting them myself." And in the last *New Masses* there is an excerpt from a letter he sent in which he asks, "Who the hell cares about Dreiser anyway?" Who cares? I'll answer that: every man who is grateful for his magnificent fight for civil liberties and the debt which everyone of us owes to him. His evasions in regard to his stand on the Jews I sharply disapprove but I am entirely out of patience with these smug Marxists who set themselves as the final judges of everything under the sun.

Don't get the notion that I have fascist leanings. Though my income is, as I told you, about $700 a year, and I have to put two sons in school away from home, yet I bought ten of the Spivak pamphlets and sent them to persons with fascist tendencies; I have recently made a contribution (small, of course) to the Herndon fund; and I wrote a year ago to the editors of *New Masses* telling them to count on me in every way I can serve in the fight against fascism and war. But I am a realist, not a romantic self-pitying person with smug notions of his own unselfishness and justice and mercy.

I tell you that many of these Marxist leaders in this country would show up as sorry and evasive shysters if a good psychological analysis were to lay them bare. I have close friends who are Marxists: I cannot tell you why they are Marxists but I do declare that if I were to tell you, the reasons would amaze you. To hell with evasions. I'm a radical, yes; but I go so damned much farther than Marxists in my revolutionary concepts that their patched-up romantic program wearies me. Wade in and be entirely candid: you can't offend me. I know you're just the sort of person I should hold in high esteem if I were to know you but I want you to meet my arguments with logic and not with romantic piffle.

Sincerely,

Vardis Fisher

EPILOGUE

EPILOGUE

Although my life has exceeded the biblical allotment of three-score years and ten, I have no intention of giving up. One of the things I would greatly love to do is to fill a gap in this book of which I am much aware. That would be to show a greater preoccupation with books and authors of the period. I do mention some of the writers and their books with whom I was involved, like Faulkner, Hemingway, Fisher, etc., but that is merely skimming the top. Nowhere do I indicate how deeply I was immersed in the books of the time. Reading was an obsession with me always. Yet I fear that this element, in my almost seventy years of reading, has been neglected in these pages.

Also, these were the years in which the book business experienced many revolutionary upheavals. The booksellers fought for the privilege of returning unsold stock—not as a favor, but as their right—and they won this battle with the publishers. We fought the discounters, and won. Then the paperbacks. They became a large part of the inventory of every bookstore. This, together with hardbound books, made it necessary for bookstores to carry larger stocks. Consequently it required more capital to enter bookselling. This lack of capital prevented the small stores from expanding and indeed forced many of them out of business. Meanwhile the chains increased and prospered. Although many problems remain unsolved, some progress has been made. Observing bookselling from a perspective which I have not had previously, I can assert that Bookselling contains hopes of surviving.

And this is the right place to report that I am leaving the bookshop in the strong capable hands of my son David. If anyone was literally "born in a bookshop," he was. That the shop will be carried on in the old tradition, I have no doubt, and he has already opened several new paths in bookselling. He has remodeled the formerly unused basement into a large, attractive Paperback Gallery. Then he went on to expand to a vacant store next door (once our original shop), which he has filled with Bargains of all sorts, from paperbacks to imported Art Books. He has the only store of its kind in the state of Wisconsin. It is unique. All the books are new and all are Bargains at half-price or less. We call it our Third Floor.

APPENDIX

The following letters represent our fledgling attempts at publicity. We were always aware of the value of PR and, besides our own efforts, attempted to get it wherever we could. Also, remember that printing and postage were inexpensive and we fired off letters at the drop of a hat. As an example, 500 of No. 2 were multigraphed for $3.75 and mailed for $7.50. One thousand of No. 3 were multigraphed for $4.75 and mailed for $13.80.

ℭ𝔞𝔰𝔞𝔫𝔬𝔳𝔞

new . old and rare books
objects of art
591 DOWNER AVE.
MILWAUKEE, WISCONSIN, U. S. A.

October 18, 1927.

Dear Madam:

We beg to announce the opening of an exclusive
Book and Art Shop.

You will not find another Book Shop in the city
more satisfactory in atmosphere, more unique in
equipment or more complete in the variety of
good books.

In addition to the book section there will be a
Circulating Library which will contain the
latest books as they are issued by the publishers.

With our collection of first editions and prints
we will carry a distinctive assortment of cards
for every occasion.

There will also be a section devoted to East
Indian art goods imported from the Vale of Kashmir;
a stock of Moroccan, Spanish and Italian pottery
and Slavic peasant ware.

Assuring you of courteous attention, we earnestly
solicit your inspection and patronage.

We are, Madam,

Yours faithfully,

CASANOVA

books and libraries purchased and appraised

No. 1. This was the first Announcement of our Opening. 500 were mailed
on October 18, 1927.

TEL. LAKESIDE 680

CASANOVA

new . old and rare books
objects of art

591 DOWNER AVE.
MILWAUKEE, WISCONSIN, U. S. A.   March 1928

Dear Madame:

We announced our opening in October; our splendid progress in November;
we were too busy to announce anything in December; and now we announce,
after two months of refurbishing and enlarging our stock, three new
features of value:

FOREIGN BOOKS: We have added a limited and select section of modern and
standard French and German literature including the names
of such eminent writers as Paul Bourget, Julien Green,
Romaine Rolland, etc., among the French; and Lion Feucht-
wanger, Schnitzler, Wassermann, etc., among the German.

MAGAZINES: Our selection of magazines has been thought of as a matter
of quality rather than quantity. Here you will find the
DIAL, the BOOKMAN, the SATURDAY REVIEW OF LITERATURE, the
NEW REPUBLIC, the NEW YORKER, the AMERICAN MERCURY, ELITE
STYLES, TRAVEL, and other fine American magazines. Our
German periodicals include: DIE WOCHE, JUGEND, BERLINER
ZEITUNG and SCHERL'S. We will take your subscription for
any AMERICAN or FOREIGN periodical at publisher's prices.

CARDS, TALLIES: We wish you to become acquainted with the new CASANOVA
CARD SERVICE. Here you may purchase BIRTHDAY, WEDDING,
THANK YOU, ANNIVERSARY, SYMPATHY, FRIENDSHIP, PARTY IN-
VITATIONS and cards for numerous other occasions. These
are all of unusual design and contain appropriate senti-
ments. If you are ever looking for something different
in BRIDGE SCORES or TALLIES, general or special PLACE
CARDS, we are sure we can fill your needs. Have you
thought of EASTER CARDS or ST. PATRICK'S DAY PLACE and
TALLY CARDS? We have a beautiful selection of these.

May we say in closing that we have all the latest books for sale as well
as an enlarged circulating library due to our rapidly increasing membership; that we are importing new pieces of pottery and odds and ends for
BRIDGE PRIZES and GIFTS.

We are, Madame,

Yours faithfully,

books and libraries purchased and appraised   CASANOVA

No. 2. This was our first Newsletter. 500 were mailed March 1928.

ℭ𝔄𝔖𝔄𝔑𝔒𝔙𝔄

new • old and rare books
objects of art
591 DOWNER AVE.
MILWAUKEE, WISCONSIN, U. S. A.

May 1928

Dear Madame:

The Casanova Lending Library Department is now preparing for
its members' summer holidays. Our mail service, which is always
active, is at your command, and we shall be pleased to keep you
supplied with renting books wherever you may be sojourning in
America. Our rates for this service are identical to those for
local residents, the only additional expense being the carriage
charges both ways. Your bill will be totalled and submitted
upon your return to the city — thus saving you an annoying detail. We should be pleased to give you further information
personally.

"What To Read In Books", a sixteen page booklet printed in
Garamond Type on fine quality English finish paper of substantial weight, will be issued monthly by CASANOVA starting with
the June number. It will fit handily into a man's pocket or a
lady's bag. A selection not exceeding thirty-six titles will
appear month by month, chosen from important books just being
published, and from the outstanding books being read currently.
All of these titles will be in The CASANOVA LENDING LIBRARY and
in stock for sale. This will enable you to keep in touch with
the best new fiction and non-fiction, which will be a decided
advantage to you among your literary friends.

If you are not a member, we earnestly believe it will be to your
benefit and pleasure to become one. To those of you who are
members and know the quality and service of our Library, we are
pleased to make the above announcement concerning our new booklet which you will receive monthly, free of charge.

Yours faithfully,

CASANOVA

Tel: Lakeside 680

books and libraries purchased and appraised

No. 3. This was our first Lending Library Newsletter. 500 were
distributed May 1928.

CASANOVA

new . old and rare books
objects of art
591 DOWNER AVE.
MILWAUKEE, WISCONSIN, U. S. A.

September 1928

To Casanovists — Members — And those who Will Be:

We take not too great pleasure in announcing our removal to 585 Downer Avenue
on the dark and memorable night of August first. On this night passers-by
were amazed and amused to see some dozen disciples of CASANOVA wending their
merry way to the new and spacious quarters thirty-nine paces (how well we
know them) south of the old stand, their arms loaded with books of every description. And here you will now find us.

From the depths of the Dark Chamber the following host of announcements come
trooping forth to light:

1. In regard to the library which is assuming vast proportions: There is
   to be no request that you renew your membership yearly. (There are
   many that would soon expire.) We have decided that your initial deposit
   of one dollar is all we shall ask of you. Once a member - always a member. You may live in Paris, Singapore or San Francisco for years, but
   on returning to Milwaukee you will still be able to draw the latest fiction and non-fiction from the CASANOVA LENDING LIBRARY without a new deposit......With what pleasure our Library Members will receive the next
   announcement: Library fees have been reduced as follows - $2.50 books:
   15¢ the first three days or 25¢ thereafter for the first week, 3¢ each
   day over the week. $3.00 books or over: 25¢ the first three days or 40¢
   thereafter for the first week, 5¢ each extra day over the week. We trust
   that our members are cognizant of the fact that we calculate fees EXCLUSIVE
   of the day you borrow the book, hence you keep it four days for the price
   of three and eight days for the cost of seven.

2. We are now carrying a stock of American and Foreign magazines that is
   double our former supply and are receiving subscriptions for any magazine
   published.

3. Our advance Christmas Personal Card line is now beautifully sampled and
   on display. We are taking orders for twenty-five or more and will make
   your engraved name plate if you can not furnish one.

Faithfully,

Lakeside 680

CASANOVA.

books and libraries purchased and appraised

No. 4. We were almost one year old. We mailed 500 in September 1928.

Casanova

MILWAUKEE, WISCONSIN, U. S. A.

new, old and rare books

first editions

A BRIEF CHECK LIST OF FIRST EDITIONS

NOTE: All books on this list are perfect save when otherwise described. Although but one title is listed of
any one author, we carry many others in stock.

❉❉❉❉❉❉❉❉❉❉❉❉❉❉❉❉❉❉❉❉❉❉❉❉❉

ANDERSON. The New Testament. 1927. Mint.	$ 2.00
BROMFIELD. Strange Case Miss Annie Spragg. 1928. Mint.	2.50
BYRNE. Destiny Bay. 1928. Mint.	3.50
BENET. John Brown's Body. 1928. Mint.	5.00
CATHER. Alexander's Bridge. 1912. Lacks front fly leaf. In dust jacket, and otherwise fine copy.	12.50
CABELL. Something About Eve. 1927. Mint.	3.50
HUNEKER. Iconoclasts. 1905. Bookplate of former owner torn from inside cover, otherwise good copy.	5.00
HERGESHEIMER. Linda Condon. 1919.	5.00
JAMES. Two Magics. 1898.	5.00
KILMER. The Circus and Other Essays. 1916. Mint.	2.50
LEWIS. Main Street. 1920. Slightly shaken. Name of former owner on front fly leaf.	6.00
LEONARD. Aesop And Hyssop. 1912.	4.50
MILLAY. Buck In The Snow. 1928. Mint.	5.00
MACHEN. Things Near And Far. 1923. One of 100 copies printed on Large Paper, signed by Machen.	25.00
MOORE. Coming of Gabrielle. 1920. One of 1,000 copies printed on Large Paper, signed by Moore.	15.00
NATHAN. Peter Kindred. 1919.	5.00
NATHAN. GEORGE, J. Bottoms Up. 1917.	3.00
NEWTON. Amenities of Book Collecting. 1918. With Errata slip on pp. 268.	25.00
ROBINSON. Avon's Harvest. 1921. Mint.	5.00
SALTUS. Daughters Of The Rich. 1909. Mint.	5.00
SEABROOK. Adventures in Arabia. 1927. 2nd. Ed. Signed and dated by Seabrook.	10.00
SUCKLING. Love Poems. 1906. One of 20 copies on Japan Vellum, printed at Torch Press. Inscribed by Editor.	5.00
WYLIE. Mr. Hodge And Mr. Hazard. 1928. Mint.	2.50

books and libraries purchased and appraised

No. 5. Our first Checklist of First Editions. We mailed 1,000 in December 1928.

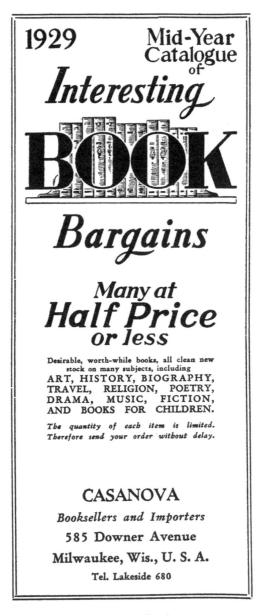

1929 Mid-Year
Catalogue
of

Interesting

BOOK

Bargains

Many at
Half Price
or less

Desirable, worth-while books, all clean new
stock on many subjects, including
ART, HISTORY, BIOGRAPHY,
TRAVEL, RELIGION, POETRY,
DRAMA, MUSIC, FICTION,
AND BOOKS FOR CHILDREN.

*The quantity of each item is limited.
Therefore send your order without delay.*

CASANOVA

Booksellers and Importers

585 Downer Avenue

Milwaukee, Wis., U. S. A.

Tel. Lakeside 680

No. 6. Our first Bargain Catalog. 1,000 were
distributed and it was not successful,
but we broke even.

CASANOVA

BOOKSELLERS

2611 N. DOWNER AVENUE

October 1932

Dear Library Member:

It has been a long time since we have written one of our informal letters, and many patrons have inquired why we have discontinued them. Our business has grown so large and multiform that it is almost impossible to devote the time we previously did to our gossipy notes. Now, however, there are so many important things to tell you about, that it is doubtful if they all can be crowded into one letter.

First, we wish to tell you about our Lending Library Delivery Service. Beginning Oct. 1st, we will deliver library books to any part of the city. Think of it! All you have to do is phone the shop (Lakeside 0680) for the book you want, and it will be delivered to you. No additional membership fee; no increase in fees; no extra charge for delivery. All books up to $3.00 will rent at 25¢ per week; all books over $3.00 will rent at 40¢ per week. Pay the driver when he delivers the book. Catalogs (Books of the Month) will be delivered free every month. Write the new books you want to read on the business reply card and mail to us or hand to driver. If you would like more information about this, please call us, or stop into the shop.

News Items:- We have successfully concluded our reorganization sale and regret that one of our directors, Mr. Paul Romaine, has left us to open his own shop. Our shop has been completely redecorated and rearranged. Some of the finest Xmas cards we have ever sold will soon be on display. Let us have your orders now, for your Personal Cards while the selection is complete. We intend to stock books of lasting quality only from now on and ignore the cheap and meretricious. May we suggest your next book gift? Mr. H. W. Schwartz will begin a series of weekly informal talks on books and writers sometime in October. If you are interested in attending these, please leave your name at the shop. We have many new plans but these will have to wait for another letter.

Faithfully yours,

Casanova

No. 7. Our partnership was dissolved and this was my first Newsletter as sole owner. Mailed 1,275 in October 1932.